LIVERPOOL BANK ROBBER TO HOLLYWOOD BUTLER

MY LIFE WITH CLINT EASTWOOD, ELIZABETH TAYLOR AND GEORGE SEGAL

TERRY MOOGAN

SPELLING DIFFERENCES: UK V US

This book was written in British English, hence US readers may notice some spelling differences from American English: e.g. color = colour, meter = metre and jewelry = jewellery

DEDICATION

To my daughter, Kelly, who has sustained me during my darkest hours and brought me the greatest joy of my life

CONTENTS

AUTHOR'S NOTE

We were never young. We were too afraid of ourselves. No one told us who we were or what we were, or where all of our parents went. Mine would arrive like ghosts, visiting me briefly, and then they'd disappear for weeks or months or years, leaving me alone with my memories and dreams, with no answers to my questions, and in complete confusion.

So begins my life story, my memoir of resilience, revelation, revulsion and finally redemption. Born into poverty in Liverpool, United Kingdom, one of the country's most infamous and dangerous places, I spent most of my childhood in so-called Approved Schools, detention centers, and Her Majesty's prisons. I escaped three times and was twice recaptured in my struggle to find stability in a world that was constantly chaotic and brutal.

Us "Scousers" as Liverpool lads like me are called, formed ourselves into street gangs to survive the harsh realities of our young lives, when the only way to scrape along was to steal, usually food or the money to buy it. While we considered bravery a top priority, we held the line at violence. All we needed was a meal a day. To get it, we took on local bullies and Borstal scum in our fight for justice and for people like us.

I believe I represent a bygone era that I hope never returns, despite the evil that is around us. With God's help, I became strong enough to turn my life around.

This is my story of that success.

I'M ONLY TEN YEARS OLD
AN INNOCENT CHILD

The courts have sentenced me to pay
In the abuser's hands I must stay
I'm in a dormitory at night
Within the abuser's sight

Thirty years have passed me by
I'm not in the abuser's sight
Why do I still cry?
It's because my fears are still so clear
Please, God, help me through the night

No more walks to the office
No more whacks of Hickey's cane
When the abusers ring the bell
Grab your coat and get out of "HELL"
Their intention was not English or French
Their intention was something else

I ran so far to get away
It's been thirty years and haunts me to this day
They've made me sick
It's the doctors who know and have the last say
It will be with me till my dying day

I see their faces wherever I go
They are doing "It" to some child I don't know
Of course they are, they don't teach English or French
Their intentions are something else
The facts are coming in thirty years too late
It's time for them to face their fate

Oh, God, I asked you to take me
When I was sick and weak
I'm glad you met me and said to me, "No!"
That I must go back and deliver my message
For all of them to know.

CHAPTER 1
SPRING, 1964, LIVERPOOL, ENGLAND

On an early morning in the summer of 1963, in the town of Ledburn in Buckinghamshire, England, a gang of 15 men waited nervously at the Bridego railway bridge. They'd tampered with the lineside signals and hoped their handiwork would bring the approaching Royal Mail train to a halt. It did just that, and within seconds, the men, led by Bruce Reynolds, boarded the train in a successful attempt at confiscating numerous bags full of cash bearing Her Majesty's crest, on their way to London.

The train driver, Jack Mills, was the only man injured in the robbery. He was hit over the head with a metal pipe and incapacitated, after initially failing to comply with the robbers' instructions. Even though he survived, he never made a full physical recovery and was never able to work again.

The gang of 15 escaped that day with over £2.5 million, making their haul the single largest robbery in British history. This would thereafter be forever known as The Great Train Robbery.

The majority of the people of Britain were horrified by the robbery. When, one by one, the culprits were arrested, the tabloids sang the praises of the heroic police and the public sang with them. There was, however, an underclass of people who idolized these men; young men who'd known nothing but poverty and wanted out of their pitiful existence, by any means necessary. They saw The Great Train Robbers as heroes, modern-day Robin Hoods, who were depriving the rich of just a fraction of what the rich had deprived us of, and were graciously doling it out to the have-nots, the nobodies who were actually ourselves.

We were a part of the latter group, but there were only five in the gang that I headed up from the age of eight. I planned our first job meticulously. I'd been observing the daily operations of The Cooperative Group supermarket, affectionately known as "The Co-op" for weeks. There was no use robbing a bank. The people of my neighborhood rarely deposited money there. They lived week-to-week or, in my case, hour to hour. Most of the wages, benefits and pensions were paid out in cash on Thursdays and handed over to the Co-op cashier, in exchange for groceries, cigarettes and booze on Fridays.

By the time this particular Friday evening came around, the old, wooden Co-op till was bursting with cash. The plan was simple, as most of the best plans are. Ronnie Gibbons, John James and David Hook stood watch as my faithful lieutenants, while Frannie Jones distracted the cashier with a friendly query.

"Excuse me, miss," he said, "can you tell me where the tins of baked beans are?"

The cashier nodded, and without thought, stepped out from behind her desk and walked casually down the center aisle, with Frannie just a step behind her. My heart was beating faster than ever before. I could feel my knees shaking. My eyes darted between the cash register and Frannie. The moment he turned and frantically nodded in my direction, I instinctively reacted. I dived over the desk and effortlessly pulled open the till.

The drawer was stacked with cash. I pulled out as many of the bank notes as I could with my shaking hands and stuffed them into my satchel. I walked briskly away from the counter, through the front door, and down the street. Ronnie, John and David laughed with excitement when they saw me. When I turned and saw Frannie on my heels, right behind me, I knew we'd gotten away with it.

We kept a fast, but steady pace, zigzagging down side streets, constantly moving through the old, decaying city, hoping we weren't being followed. Finally, we got to the only place I felt was safe enough to rest: Anfield Cemetery. I peeled off ten pounds from the haul and buried the rest in the same unkempt corner of the graveyard I'd been using to hide all the money I'd procured through my various, nefarious schemes.

We made our way to the nearest off-license; a small, dingy liquor store, just a few minutes' walk from the graveyard. I bought five cigars and a box of matches, gave one to each of the lads, and we puffed away happily, without a care in the world.

I flagged down a taxi. We hopped in and I asked the driver to take us across the water to the posh, exciting shopping district of New Brighton. We all jumped out of the taxi when we arrived and I leaned back in to pay the driver.

"Did you rob The Co-op?" he asked with a furrowed brow.

"No," I replied.

I ushered the others out towards the shops and restaurants and, although he didn't follow us, I knew the driver was up to something.

In the evening, we took the ferry back to the city, and when we reached the docks, we were greeted by six policemen, who towered over us. We were arrested for burglary. John, Ronnie and David were all given probation, but Frannie Jones and I were released with no action. We were, after all, only nine years old. Up until this time, I'd been quite lucky in my schemes and had collected a small fortune from the business of larceny. I knew things could potentially be bad for me if I were caught again, but I had no idea how bad it would get.

CHAPTER 2
URCHIN CHILD

I was born in February 1957, in Liverpool City Centre, on the notorious Scotland Road of Hard Knocks. I was the youngest of seven children. We all lived in a two-bedroom, middle-floor flat in a dismal, concrete, high-rise tenement. It was just one of many tenements that filled the horizons of the decrepit council estates of the cities of Northern England.

The elevator, which Brits call the lift, was oftentimes not working, and even when it was, it constantly smelled like urine, obviously the result of the many degraded drunks, who couldn't hold it long enough to make it to their flats. The other inhabitants, our neighbors, just didn't care and neither did we. The sound of glass smashing, men shouting in rage, and women and children screaming with fear, was pervasive to the point of seeming normal to my siblings and me.

My father, Patrick Moogan, was in the Merchant Navy and constantly absent. My mother, Frances, did her best to raise us. Dad sent his wages home, but it just wasn't enough. Mum struggled to stay financially afloat, working part-time in the Hartley Jam factory. The stress of raising seven children, her back-breaking, low-paid job, and having no money to properly feed and clothe us took a desperate toll on her psyche. She'd become mentally frail.

By the winter of 1963, my survival instincts kicked in and I decided to go out and make it on my own. I was seven years old and couldn't be tamed. The local school authorities were constantly harassing my mother about my absence from school. She tried to explain to them that she was in over her head but, instead of offering help and guidance, the harassment increased, leading her to descend deeper and deeper into depression and desperation.

She tried keeping me in the flat. In the evenings, she'd tuck me into her bed, right next to her, on the side furthest away from the door, but it didn't help. I'd just wake up before her, sometimes before daybreak, and leave without her knowing. I'd only ever return late at night to sleep.

There were many others just like me. I was a child of the streets, an urchin. I needed to find a job. I was sick and tired of not having food in my belly and wearing rags instead of decent, warm clothes.

One day, in the bitterly cold winter, I awoke at the witching hour, three o'clock in the morning, and trekked to the outskirts of the city. I stood, shivering, outside the giant gates of

Fresh Field Farm, and waited for the milkman. At exactly four o'clock, the gates creaked open and two majestic Shire horses gracefully trotted out. They were pulling a massive cart. It was packed with stacked crates, full of fresh milk and juice bottles. Stan, the milkman, was in the driver's seat, pulling the reins.I could see he was shocked by the sight of me.

"What are you doing here, lad?" he asked. The tone of his voice seemed concerned and paternal.

"I need a job."

He looked me dead in the eyes, and without missing a beat, he said, "Jump on."

I knew he was impressed by my attitude. Many of the street kids worked by running the milk for the many milkmen employed by the farm, but few waited outside, long before the crack of dawn, for the chance of a job. I worked with Stan every day that week. I was fast and eager to please, sprinting to the various houses and diligently placing the milk bottles on the steps of the customers' doors, careful not to wake them with the noise, or inadvertently break a bottle here and there. Stan would give me a bottle of milk and a bottle of juice every day and promised to pay me at the end of the week.

Sometimes, I'd drop my bottle of milk off at home but, most

of the time, I just drank it to fill my empty belly. On Friday, at the end of the first week, Stan asked me if I'd help him collect the money from the customers for the milk he'd delivered the previous week. I was only too happy to help. He took me to each house and introduced me to the customers. They each paid him cash. He stashed the money in his apron and checked them off in his little pocketbook.

He paid me half a crown, directly from the weekly total. I flipped the coin in my hand and pondered what I was going to buy with it. It was enough to pay for a loaf of bread and half a dozen eggs, with a little left over for a bar of chocolate or some other sweet treat, but it wasn't by any means enough to survive on. A plan was beginning to hatch in my mind's eye.

The next week, I worked just as hard as I'd worked before. I sprinted to every house and took time to care for the needs of the customer. I even helped Stan with the horses and loaded the crates on the cart at the beginning of each shift. By the time Friday rolled around, I arrived at each of the customers' houses approximately one hour before Stan and I had arrived the previous week and I collected the cash.

The customers had already been introduced to me and therefore handed over the loot without a second thought. Most even complimented me on my work ethic. I collected £36 that day, which was the equivalent of a month's wages for most people in the neighborhood. I stuffed the money into my satchel and ran off to the peaceful surroundings of Anfield Cemetery, where I buried the cash in my usual neglected corner of the graveyard. I'd stolen things before, such as food, coins and chocolate from the local shops, but this was the first time I actually planned a caper. Many more were to come.

CHAPTER 3
CAPTURED IN THE WEB OF ABUSE

By the middle of 1966, our little gang was making quite an impact. Our Friday night robberies continued to go off without a hitch. We were now diversifying and robbing not only the supermarkets, but also the local off-licenses (liquor stores) and tobacconists. Some of the gang would burglarize houses in the neighborhood, but not me. I knew the majority of the inhabitants of the estate we lived on survived week to week. Not only did they not have much to steal, but the idea of taking anything from them, no matter how little, just didn't seem right to me.

The lads and I would often sit together and plan our next criminal enterprise. One evening, David Hook devised a plan that would've netted us a small fortune. Although he was a Protestant, he began going to mass on Sunday mornings and watching as the local parishioners would deposit money into a wooden box under the candle stand. The candle stand housed hundreds of small tea-light candles. Parishioners would light a candle, place it on the stand, and say a small prayer for one of their deceased family members. They would then deposit a coin in the candle box below the stand or into the donation box for the church.

Sunday was obviously the most productive day for the church. The last mass of the day was in the late afternoon, but the church wasn't locked up until after 8 pm. David proposed that he and John should be the lookouts, while Frannie and I smashed the locks off the donation and candle boxes and then poured the loot into plastic grocery bags, before making a swift getaway. I listened quietly to the plan but, inside, my blood was boiling.

David was unaware how much we Liverpool Irish Catholics venerated the church. I told him I would have no part in his plan and warned him that, if he even attempted the robbery, I'd give him a severe beating. David ignored my threat and robbed the church with the help of another group of street kids. I was livid. In the confrontation that ensued, I beat him into submission and left him in a pool of his own blood.

David was no longer a part of our gang and we parted as enemies. Years later, when I was in my late teens, I heard that David had been the victim of a fire at school. He was smoking with another boy, Brian Steel, in the loft when a group of children from a nearby psychiatric institution set fire to the school. David and Brian were trapped, and when the fire brigade finally rescued them, both boys had extensive lung damage. Brian sustained third-degree burns over 90 percent of his body, while David suffered with third-degree burns over 75 percent of his body. I visited David in hospital and we eventually became friends again.

David was out, but the rest of the gang were as strong and as active as ever. We had a winning formula when it came to robbing supermarkets, so we extended the caper to the bingo halls. Twice a week, Broadway Cinema became a bingo hall. Friday was by far the busiest night of the week. The place would be packed to the point of bursting with seniors and old age pensioners, many of the women with blue and pink hair rinses. They arrived armed with a stack of colored pens and just enough money to buy their bingo card and splurge on a cheeky gin and tonic to calm their overly competitive nerves.

When everyone was seated and ready to play and the wooden cash register was full to the brim, John and Ronnie would keep watch on the front doors. Frannie would distract the cashier with a concession inquiry and I would reach into the cash register and grab every bank note I could before bolting out into the street.

The following week, I devised a plan to rob the Mother's Pride Bread Company. The bakery had delivery men who would deliver bread to the various housing estates and sell it straight from the van. Frannie and I were to get work helping the delivery drivers. We used exactly the same tactics as I had with the milkman.

Frannie and I would work with different deliverymen, gain their trust, and then steal whatever we could.

I thought the plan would take longer than it did but, in the first week, the deliveryman collected all the cash and then drove to the bakery. He left me in the passenger seat of the van and told me to "keep an eye on that," as he exited the van and casually walked into the bakery, leaving his leather satchel, containing all the cash and his wallet, on the driver's seat. I got Frannie's attention and ordered him to check the seats of all the other bread vans, in the hope that just a few more deliverymen had made a similar mistake. Frannie came up empty-handed but, when we ran off to Anfield Cemetery and counted the loot, we were overjoyed at becoming £36 wealthier.

Our next caper was the most lucrative yet. Most of the houses in the estate contained an electricity and a gas meter under the stairs. Each meter housed a cash box, locked with a padlock. To keep the utilities working, the residents had to constantly feed the meter with 10-pence coins, which would later be replaced by 50-pence coins.

The strategy was simple enough. I reasoned that, by only targeting the utility cash boxes, I could burglarize a house without depriving the tenants of anything.

We made it through a few houses, stashing the coins in our signature plastic grocery bags, and when the bags were too full or when we feared them bursting at the seams, we'd stash the rest in our pockets and leave a trail of the swag out of the house.

One day, we watched a row of houses until a middle-aged woman left her house and locked the door. She checked that the door was locked by pulling on the door handle a few times, and when she was satisfied that the house was secured, she walked up the street and out of sight. We waited a few more minutes, and when we were sure she wouldn't return, we made our move. We ran to the back of the house, out of view of the street, and broke in by smashing the kitchen window and lifting the latch. We made a bit of noise, but we were satisfied the house was unoccupied, so it didn't matter to us at the time.

We got to the stairs and began the process. Frannie stood behind me with the bag as I pushed the head of a screwdriver into the hinge of the utility box and began banging the handle with a hammer. It was then that we heard a voice from the stairs and the sound of footsteps pounding on each step. I ran for the window and scrambled through it.

All I heard behind me was an angry male voice screaming, "Come here, you little bastard!"

I landed on the ground and instantly began running, without looking back. Frannie was nowhere to be seen. He'd been caught. Apparently, the husband of the woman we'd seen leave the house was fast asleep in bed when we'd entered the house. The sound of the screwdriver being hammered into the box woke him out of his slumber and alerted him to our presence. Frannie was gone, but I'd evaded capture yet again. The rest of us in the gang carried on as usual. I thought I was free and clear.

One early morning in May 1967, there was a forceful knock on the door of our flat. My mother answered the door to two detectives from the Liverpool Constabulary's Criminal Investigation Division. Without hesitation, they arrested me for burglary, took me to The Menlove Avenue Assessment Centre and placed me there on remand until the courts decided my fate.

I had lived on the harsh, cold, violent streets for years and thought I was ready for anything, but this place was like hell on Earth. It seemed to be set up to be harsh. The noise was persistent. Young boys would scream and scuffle in the night and the red night light hanging from the ceiling would keep me awake. I was suffering from sleep deprivation and anxiety, due to the violent nature of the place. The bullying was constant, as were the fights. Day in and day out, I kept my head on a swivel and lived in constant fear of being attacked, either by the other inmates or the adult teachers, who were charged with our care.

In court, I was found guilty of burglary and sentenced under Section 1948 of the Children's Act. The act made it clear that, if a child aged ten years or older committed an offense as egregious as mine, he could be interred in the "Approved School" system for a period of time to be determined by a judge. I was sentenced to three years. That's when I realized the police knew all along that I was Frannie's accomplice in the burglary, but had waited until after my tenth birthday to arrest me, so I could be well and truly locked away at Her Majesty's pleasure.

The evening of my conviction, I was taken back to Menlove Avenue to begin the process of preparing to be moved to an approved school. It was then that I realized I had to escape. With the help of another prisoner, we hatched a plan. We waited until the early hours of the morning and began tying our sheets together into a makeshift rope. We tied the rope to a steel bar on the wall and smashed the window. We threw the sheets out of the window, scaled down them and ran from the grounds of the center.

Menlove Avenue was in quite an opulent suburb of Liverpool. Its most famous resident at the time was John Lennon. We didn't belong in the neighborhood and stuck out like a sore thumb. Before long, we saw the ominous sight of two mounted police officers, trotting down the road towards us. There was nowhere for us to go, nowhere to escape to. We succumbed to our fate and surrendered immediately.

We were taken back to the remand center, given pajamas to wear, and locked alone in a tiny room containing a bed, a sink and a toilet in the Secure Unit of the facility. We spent three days there, and during that time, we were given nothing but bread and water to eat and drink. I spent two more weeks in that facility before being told I was being transferred to St. George's Approved School, situated on the outskirts of Liverpool. I hated the remand center and was happy to be leaving, but nothing could've prepared me and the countless others for the horrific web of abuse we were about to endure at the hands of the Catholic Church.

CHAPTER 4
ST. GEORGE'S APPROVED SCHOOL

In June 1967, still aged ten years old, I was taken into a stark room at the Menlove Avenue Remand Centre. The only items of furniture in the room were a table, which was bolted to the ground, and a chair. I was told to sit down. After the door slammed shut, I was left to my own thoughts for what seemed like hours.

I began to nod off, and just as I closed my eyes, the door opened violently. It slammed into the wall behind it and two men walked in. This was serious. They were big and looked hard as nails. Even though they weren't wearing uniforms, I knew they were coppers. The first man through the door looked me straight in the eyes and scowled.

"Stand up and hold out your hands," he said in a stern and demanding tone.

I complied. Then, without saying another word, he pulled a pair of handcuffs from a pouch behind his back and clipped them tightly to my wrists. They were heavy and I mean really heavy. Each cuff weighed approximately three pounds. With his colleague right behind him, he pulled me out of the room, down the stairs, and into the courtyard, where an armored, navy-blue police van, a "Black Mariah," awaited us. They opened the back doors and lifted me into the back, then unceremoniously slammed the door. Hard.

As the van began to move, I sat on one of the two parallel benches that were bolted to the right and left sides of the van. It was claustrophobic, windowless, and dark. The only light came from the heavily fortified caged window leading to the front seats of the van.

The journey didn't last long. Within 15 minutes, the van came to a halt and the back doors swung open. The coppers reached in, grabbed me by the arm and pulled me from the van.

There, right in front of me, was a massive red brick building. I'd arrived at St. George's Approved School for boys, in the quaint and prosperous neighborhood of Freshfields. It was surrounded by beautiful, lush fields filled with trees, but the building itself was ominous and reminded me of a prisoner-of-war camp. As I was led through the large wooden door, a sense of foreboding, the likes of which I'd never felt before, struck me.

We walked just a few steps and came to an office door. I could hear children playing outside and the loud echoing click of leather-soled shoes on the tiled floors. The place smelled sterile, a combination of pine disinfectant and the old wood and dust smell of an aged church.

The office door opened and out walked a man, who introduced himself as Mr. Carroll. He was short and rotund, with a plump belly and jet-black hair. He was menacing and stern. He spoke out of the side of his mouth, with the resonance of a regimental sergeant major. He glibly chatted with the cops and apologized to them for the inconvenience of having to waste their time on a delinquent like me. A few minutes passed by and the polite chatting stopped when we were approached by a giant of a man. The two cops were big, heavily built men, but this guy towered over them.

He was 6 ft 7 and weighed in at approximately 270 lbs. His hands were as big as shovels and his hair was ginger. He was Mr. Mathews, a former Irish Guard. There were five houses at the school, each containing about 30 boys and Mr. Mathews was the head of St. Mary's House. He thanked the police and Mr. Carroll for waiting, and after the police took the handcuffs off my wrists, Mr. Mathews told me to follow him.

He walked me silently up a staircase to a dormitory with beds lining two long walls. He showed me to my bed and instructed me to change into my uniform, which was waiting for me on the bed. I did as I was told. The whole place was set up to be a school to teach us the basics of life and a reformatory to transform us into decent, Christian citizens, but that wasn't the reality.

The place was, instead, a sadist's dream. Every day, we'd be marched to the doors of the main hall, where we'd attend assembly. While standing in line waiting, boys would be randomly pulled out of the line for *talking*. Their punishment was both humiliating and painful. The child would be told to stand in a position of attention and raise his right cheek. He would them be slapped on the right side of his face, at full force, five times. The process would then be repeated on the left side.

Eventually, we'd be led into the main hall and ordered to sit on the floor in huddled rows. We'd recite prayers and be given pertinent information about the upcoming school day. At the end, Mr. Carroll would call out the names of the children who were going to be punished for their "transgressions" of the previous day. Those children would be ordered to the Headmaster, Mr. Hickey's office, where they would be punished at his discretion.

As the days went on, my heart grew cold. I was distant and had to keep my guard up all the time. We were each given a range of chores to do every day. I was made to scrub the red tiled floor of a hallway with a toothbrush and then polish it with a cloth until it shone. Then I had to clean the toilets in the same manner. If the task wasn't done to Mr. Mathews' standard, I would be made to do it again.

Mealtimes were when you really had to watch your back. We'd sit in the dining hall at long tables, in seats we were assigned. Teapots full of piping hot tea were placed at intervals down the table, so that each child could get his share. Vernon, an evil bully of a child from Manchester, sat opposite me, and Victor Peel sat next to me during mealtimes. One day, after an argument, Vernon took the lid off the teapot and poured the whole thing over Victor's head, who was then sent in an ambulance to a nearby hospital, with scalding burns covering his head, back and shoulders. I never saw him again. The teachers didn't see the incident, only the aftermath. None of the boys informed on Vernon; it was just something we didn't do, an unwritten law of the underclass. The whole thing was brushed aside as a tragic accident.

A few days later, Victor tried it again, but with me this time. I knocked the teapot out of his hand and punched him senseless. I was caught red-handed by Mathews and was punished with the usual five slaps on each side of the face.

It paid to be tough at St. George's and it paid to sleep with one eye open. Many of the boys would be afflicted with night terrors. Some would sleepwalk and frantically pull on the emergency doors, in a half-catatonic attempt to escape. Some would talk and even scream in their sleep. Mr. Mathews' bedroom was at the end of our dormitory. At least twice a week, he would wake us at three o'clock in the morning, by standing in the middle of the dormitory and clapping his hands.

He'd pull a random child from his bed and explain to the rest of us that he'd been heard talking and that, as a result, we were all going to be punished. He'd march us down the stairs to the showers and order us to undress and shower in freezing cold water. He'd stand there watching our naked bodies until he was well and truly satisfied and then order us to back to our beds.

The quiet, docile boys would often be woken late at night, when Mr. Mathews thought we were all sleeping. He'd choose one and take the boy to his room. He'd soften them up with treats, such as chocolate, candy and cocoa, and then rape them and send them back to their beds, where they would whimper and cry themselves to sleep. Often, their sheets would be stained with blood. He didn't try this with kids like me. I was too much of a handful, a loose cannon. They all preferred the kids they knew would never resist.

The horror never ended. If it wasn't the teachers attacking us, it was the other students. We would fight on the playground. Some of the weaker boys were so terrified that they would defecate in their pants. I was known for violence, and as a result, I was separated from the other children and made to pull weeds and dig in the *allotment*, the vegetable garden across the courtyard from the main school building.

The winters were the worst. We would all be made to line up outside in the freezing cold. Our fingers and lips would chafe and we'd try in vain to stay still, but the shivering always got the better of us. After a long period of stillness, we'd be made to march and then run, never knowing when the ordeal would stop.

One day, I was informed by Mr. Mathews that my father had suffered a heart attack. I started my day off as usual: breakfast, assembly and then my chores. When my chores were completed, I grabbed my coat and ran to Freshfields train station. I jumped on a train and avoided the ticket collector. I got off at Bootle Strand Station and walked the two-mile journey to the hospital.

I found my father with tubes protruding from him and wires stuck to his chest. The hypnotic beep of his heart monitor filled my ears. I sat beside him for a while, and when he woke, he looked me straight in the eyes.

"What're you doing here?" he said.

I didn't answer, and instead, I asked him if he was okay. He was too weak to answer.

I left the hospital, feeling lonely. I had nobody to call on. John James was serving time at Thomas Moor's Approved School in Ainsdale, and Frannie Jones had been sentenced to time in Red Bank, a secure unit housing psychopaths and child murderers. I decided to sleep in Anfield Cemetery that night. It was bitterly cold but peaceful. My zone of sanctuary. I took some money from my buried stash to buy food and slept better than I ever had at St. George's.

The next day, as I was walking down the street, a police car approached me slowly from behind. They had been searching for me. I was arrested and taken to Walton Lane Police Station. I spent the night in the underground, dank bridewell, the nineteenth-century subterranean series of cells that seemingly hadn't ever been updated. The following afternoon, Mr. Mathews and Mr. Carroll came to collect me. They took me back and I resumed my sentence that night, as if nothing had happened.

One day later, at assembly, my name was called out. I was made to stand up in front of the whole school, while Mr. Carroll told the rest of the school my crime of absconding. It was humiliating, but not nearly as humiliating as what was about to happen. I was ordered by Mr. Carroll to go to the Headmaster, Mr. Hickey's office and wait outside the door.

I waited with my nose against the wall for what seemed like hours. Eventually, Mr. Hickey opened the door and shouted for me to enter. He closed the door behind me and told me to take down my trousers and underwear and then bend over his desk. I did as I was ordered. He caned me six times across the buttocks, with a cane measuring approximately two yards.

For the next four to six weeks, it was extremely painful to walk and sit down. My buttocks were black and blue, with welts seemingly a half-inch thick. The punishment didn't end there. For three months, I was banned from going home for my usual monthly visit, and during that period, when the other boys played on the playground, I was ordered to stand still on a painted line in the courtyard.

St. George's was a giant, sadistic, torture chamber. It was supposed to be a place of reform, but many of the children who were sentenced to time there later became bank robbers, psychopaths and killers. Just a few months after I arrived, two boys escaped through a window and down a drainpipe. They ran for their lives towards Formby Beach and were chased by both teachers and policemen. The tides were unusually high that year, but the boys kept running, and when it came to a choice between capture and the treacherous, cold sea, they chose the latter and drowned. To those boys, death was a far more merciful fate than what waited for them inside the red brick walls of St. George's.

CHAPTER 5
ONE DAY OF FREEDOM

Towards the end of 1970, Mr. Mathews came to the dorm and told me to follow him. I followed a few feet behind him, down the stairs and along the sterile corridor towards his office. The heavy click coming from his leather-soled shoes echoed as he walked, adding weight to his obvious military bearing.

My heart raced as fast as my mind as I tried to guess my immediate fate. Was I to be his next sexual abuse victim? No, I was far too much of a loose cannon for that. Was I to be beaten for some minor transgression? No, he wouldn't go to the trouble of taking me to his office for that. I had no idea what was to come and that made the short walk all the more terrifying. I was used to preparing myself for the worst these bastards had to offer, but the unknown was truly terrifying.

He opened the door and casually waved me inside. He grabbed a pile of newly-pressed clothes that were neatly stacked on his desk and thrust them at my chest. I grabbed them in my arms and stared at him in bewilderment.

"Go back upstairs and put these on. Then come back to me and make it quick," he said, without even looking in my direction.

Without another word, I ran out of his office and back to the dorm. I stripped off and put on the newly-pressed dark trousers, white shirt, blazer and shoes. I ran to his office and steadied my breathing before knocking on the door. Mr. Mathews opened the door and told me I was being released. He handed me a pass that would work on the public transport system and escorted me to the front door.

When I walked out into the cold morning air, Mathews slammed the door hard behind me. A part of me was thrilled that

I was free of this house of horrors, but another part of me was anxious as to what would come next. I had served a sentence of two years and eight months at St. George's. My body was almost three years older than it was the day I arrived there, but my brain had sustained damage from the physical and mental abuse I had been subjected to and the emotional scars had taken their toll on me. Decades later, this was proved when I was placed under the personal care of the world-renowned and prominent brain disorder specialist, Dr. Daniel Amen.

With my newfound freedom, I took the bus home to our flat on Scotland Road. The place was empty. There was no food, so I decided to do what I'd always done and return to the streets. I needed to find something to eat, so I decided to stake out some of the neighborhood houses. I jumped the fence of one house and covertly peered in the windows. When I was sure there was no-one inside, I ran around to the back of the house and broke in through the kitchen window. I ran up the stairs and rifled through the bedroom closets. I found a suitcase, took it to the kitchen and filled it with canned food from the cupboards and fresh food from the fridge. I lugged the heavy suitcase out of the house and up the street, until I came a nearby bus stop. I then sat on the bench, feeling safe in the knowledge that I would at least eat that night.

I casually glanced to my right and saw a police car moving slowly towards me. My heart sank. Myriad thoughts bounced around in my skull.

Are they looking for me? Don't act suspicious. Don't look at the coppers. Don't ignore the coppers. Should I run and leave the food? Should I run with the food? Stay calm, they'll move on.

They stopped and my heart sank. One of the neighbors of the house I had stolen from saw me leave the house and called the police. I was arrested and charged with burglary. I was once again taken to a stark, underground cell in the police station's bridewell, where I spent the night before being transferred to Menlove Avenue Remand Centre. There, I stayed for another week before being sentenced by a magistrate to another three years at St. George's.

I wasn't scared or shocked by the transportation this time. The handcuffs seemed lighter but that's because I was bigger. When I arrived, Mr. Mathews seemed surprised and he laughed at the sight of me.

"You again," he said, before showing me to the same bed I'd slept in just a few weeks before.

I stayed there for just one week. I couldn't take another three years in that asylum. One night, I waited until everyone was asleep, got dressed, climbed out of a window and slid down a drainpipe into the school grounds. I ran off into the cover of darkness and made my way back to Liverpool. I slept in Anfield Cemetery the first night. It was cold, but it was a damn sight more comfortable than St. George's. At least I could actually sleep in the cemetery, without the threat of being woken up by the insane pedophile, Mr. Mathews, or being killed in my bed by some psychotic teenager.

The next day, I saw John James in Liverpool. He told me I would be able to sleep on the couch in his mother's home and that's where I rested my head most nights thereafter. Some nights, I would sleep in the pigeon loft of another friend's home. John had also done time in the approved school system and had recently been freed.

It wasn't long before Frannie Jones joined us. Frannie had been released from Red Bank Secure Unit in Newton-le-Willows in Lancashire, an infamous asylum for the criminally insane. He was a short boy with a slight build, his hair parted at the side. He wore thick, black-framed glasses, provided graciously by the National Health Service and he constantly moved his eyes and turned his head, scanning his environment, indicative of a boy who knew from personal experience that danger was a constant in our unforgiving environment.

The gang was back together and we were up to our old tricks. Frannie and I never argued and always agreed and backed each other in our criminal undertakings. Frannie was small and looked in many ways feeble, but even most of the adults in our community were wary of him. He would catch the eye of a passerby and scream at him.

"What the fuck are you looking at?" he'd yell, and then carry on about his business, like nothing had happened.

Frannie would take risks that I would never have taken alone. He would watch women scrubbing their doorsteps in the daytime on Fridays, knowing there would be money in their purses from payday, which was always a Thursday, and that their husbands would be at work.

He'd quietly break into their kitchen at the back of their house and steal their purse, which was usually in the kitchen, due to the familiar habits of most of the women in the community. He was successful most of the time and could make good money with that particular caper. One day, he broke into a house and was met by the man of the house who, for some reason, was home from work.

"What the hell are you doing here?" said the man angrily.

Frannie just pointed at the man and said, "Uncle John, Uncle John," feigning being a simpleton, before turning and leaving the house in a hurry.

Our original caper was still our major money-maker. In the winter of 1970, John, Frannie and I decided to rob the local Woolworth's store. John was the lookout, Frannie created a distraction and lured the clerk away from the cash register, and I reached over the desk and pulled as much money as I could from the till. It was a tried and tested method, and once again, it worked. Or so we thought. A few days after the robbery, Frannie and I were caught by the police on the street. They took us to the station and set up an identity parade. The Woolworth's clerk picked us out of the line-up and we were charged once more and sent to Menlove Avenue Remand Centre.

This time, Frannie and I were imprisoned together. None of the kids in Menlove went anywhere near us, as we were far too strong for that. Frannie and I became a tight-knit pair. The staff referred to us as The Kray Twins, a reference to Ronnie and Reggie Kray, the notorious kings of the London underground during the 1960s. We would scoff at the name. After all, the Kray

Twins hadn't accomplished or even nearly been through the shit we had by the time they were our age.

Within a week, we appeared in front of a magistrate and were sentenced to three years in St. Aiden's Intermediate Approved School.

CHAPTER 6
THE HOUSE OF HORRORS

I was transported to St. Aiden's in the same manner as the two previous times I'd been sentenced to St. George's, in a Black Mariah police van. There were a few differences this time, though. I was physically bigger and stronger and I was with my mate, Frannie. We had no fear, only a deep, penetrating rage that constantly boiled in our bellies and chests. We were intent on perpetuating total mayhem in the place. The staff knew about us in advance and they thought they were prepared.

The old Victorian red-brick building was built more like a prison than a school. Before walking into it, I could feel the heavy cloak of evil being draped over my entire body. Unlike St. George's, St. Aiden's was fortified with a high brick perimeter wall, making it difficult for anyone to even attempt to escape.

I don't remember the names of the teachers. We didn't care enough to remember their names. They were harsh, just like the monsters at St. George's, where most of the teachers had their personal victims whom they'd rape countless times with impunity. We, however, were immune from that. The staff were cautious of us, possibly even scared.

It was almost impossible to sleep at night. Most of us suffered from Hyper Vigilance, a disorder which keeps the mind in a constant state of awareness, due to the violence that had been perpetuated against us. One night, after tossing and turning in his bed, Frannie, in the bed next to mine, asked me if I was awake. I told him I was and watched him as he paced the floor while pulling at his hair. He was constantly depressed and the darkness of night made his depression substantially worse.

I tried to calm him by talking him down but he continued

to pace and ramble incoherently. A boy from Manchester, who Frannie personally hated, was in the bed on the other side of him and told him to "shut the fuck up" before turning over on his side and closing his eyes in an attempt to sleep.

Frannie calmly walked back to the boy's bed, took the neatly folded clothes that were on the chair and carefully placed them on the bed. He then grabbed the chair and held it over his head before dropping it down with full force on the boy's head. Whack! Whack! Whack! He hit the boy repeatedly. The blankets and sheets the boy was wrapped in stopped any of the blood from spraying or spilling onto Frannie. Under the sheets, the boy lay still in a pool of thick, dark red, coagulated blood.

Frannie carefully set the chair back in its rightful place and draped the boy's clothes back onto it. The Night Watchman must've heard the commotion because, within minutes, he came bursting into the dorm and switched the lights on. He scanned all the beds. Most of the boys were pretending to sleep, Frannie and me included. The watchman saw the red stain seeping through the blankets of the boy next to Frannie and called for help. Shortly, more of the staff arrived and all of us were told to sit up in our beds. The boy's jaw and both arms were broken. He was transported to hospital and we never saw him again.

Frannie and I were questioned by the police. They told me they knew that I had something to do with the attack but I denied it. I just sat there with a vacant look in my eyes, a look I'd developed through years of dealing with monsters, whose constant aim was to break me. They bombarded me with accusations but I knew if I just kept quiet, they couldn't prove anything.

For a week, Frannie was kept in the dormitory in his pajamas, while the staff and police tried to sort out the situation. He denied any part of it and none of the other boys would cooperate with the authorities. No action was taken. Frannie and I went back to our routine, as if nothing had happened.

But things were getting worse and Frannie was becoming increasingly unhinged. He knew this, too, so when he told me his plan of escape while playing table tennis one night, I just nodded and went along with it. This is how it went down.

We were in the dining hall and had just taken our seats at the long tables. We were forbidden to talk at this time, so when Frannie began whispering to a boy across the table, he drew the ire of one of the teachers supervising us.

"Shut up, boy!"

Frannie stood and screamed back at the teacher.

"Who the fuck are you talking to?" he shouted at the top of his lungs.

He didn't stop there. He ran to the cutlery stand and grabbed handfuls of knives and forks. He threw them viciously at the teachers and then grabbed more and kept throwing them, until the cutlery stand was empty. The other boys then began to scream and shout. They banged their plates on the tables and began running around the room. The teachers were shocked. They had no idea what to do. They'd never been in a situation like this before. The whole place was in an uproar. Chaos engulfed the room and Frannie and I used it to our advantage.

We ran up the stairs and into the games room. We grabbed chairs and threw them through the large windows, smashing the glass to pieces and opening a path of escape. We eased out of the window frame, careful not to cut ourselves on the remaining jagged glass in the corners, and climbed down a drainpipe into the courtyard. We bolted to the perimeter wall and leapt onto it, grabbing the highest bricks and pulling ourselves up on to the top of the wall, before dropping down to the other side. The free side.

We'd made it out! Now we had to make it back to our beloved Liverpool. We walked briskly through Widnes, and when we reached the railway tracks, we followed them to Runcorn, where we waited patiently for a train.

When the train arrived, Frannie and I jumped on and hid in the toilet to avoid the conductor. He banged once on the door and asked to see a ticket. I just told him through the door that my dad had my ticket in another carriage. He didn't bother us again. We were home free now. We were back in Liverpool, sleeping in the cemetery and doing what we did best: daylight robbery.

I would eventually sue St. Aiden's in what would become the biggest lawsuit in British history at the time. It took 14 years to conclude and would be featured in a television documentary on Panorama titled, "Hear No Evil, See No Evil."

CHAPTER 7
WHISKEY HEIST ON THE DOCKS

We needed to change out of our school uniforms, so our first stop was the Army and Navy Supply Store. We each stole a pair of jeans, a denim jacket and a pair of Doc Marten boots. We didn't waste any time. We just walked right out of the shop with the merchandise. We changed behind an old pub and threw our uniforms into a nearby dumpster.

We made our way to Pier Head on the bank of the river Mersey and begged for food around the food court. We'd ask the various shoppers if they'd buy us some sausage rolls, steak and kidney pies, and cups of tea. Most of the people were kind and seemed to accept that we were genuinely hungry. Frannie and I were truly grateful to the people who helped us.

It wasn't long before we came across a local gang, led by the notorious Joe Kavanaugh. Joe was known to be as hard and tough as nails. He was the unofficial leader of a crew consisting of Richie Harrison, Egga London, Joey Wright and his good self. Joe's crew didn't want anything to do with Frannie and me, but Joe and I knew one another from the streets and had respect for each other. When we met them, they were on their way to pulling off a heist and Joe asked us if we wanted to join them. We weren't in the least bit reticent. We needed money and Joe was offering us a cut of the loot, so we followed his lead.

His plan was to break into the whiskey stores on the docks and steal whatever we could. From there, we'd somehow transport it to Joe's house, where he'd sell the whiskey and split the cash equally between us.

We walked just over a half mile to the warehouse. It looked abandoned. We looked up at the massive building for a method of entry. I spotted a number of windows high up. We found a ladder propped up at the side of the building and made our decision. We used the ladder to climb onto the roof of a nearby shed and then propped the ladder against the warehouse. Frannie climbed the ladder to the first window. He pulled off his jacket, wrapped it around his arm and then smashed the window with his fist. Within just a few minutes, we were all inside and had climbed down onto the floor of the warehouse to look around the gigantic, industrial building.

It was packed with wooden crates, filled with bottles of whiskey. We found two steel trolleys and began loading them up with the crates. The crates were so heavy that it took two of us to lift each of them. The plan was to push the trolleys to Joe's house on Scotland Road, but like all such plans, Murphy's Law raised its ugly head.

We all stopped in our tracks when we heard dogs barking. We knew it had to be the police. Someone must have heard the window breaking or seen the ladder up against the window and called it in. Our fears were proved justified when we heard the police radios as they got closer.

There was no other alternative but to run. We sprinted to the back of the building and escaped through a window. We climbed down a drainpipe, but the only way to freedom was across the Leeds and Liverpool canal. We all jumped into the water and began swimming across the freezing cold and putrid water. The weight of my clothes and boots made it difficult to swim but I was a strong swimmer, and with the bank of the canal in sight, we all pushed forward. For a split second, I glanced back and noticed that Frannie was stuck in the middle of the canal, trying desperately to keep his head above the water. He was in trouble and I knew I had to save him.

Joe and I swam to his aid. I told him not to panic, grabbed the back of his head and pulled him to safety with one hand as I swam with the other. We dragged Frannie up the bank and pulled him to his feet. Fortunately, the police were on the other side of the river from us. Their dogs were barking and the coppers shouted obscenities at us. We were so relieved at not being caught and surviving the swim that all we could do was laugh at them.

Frannie was still in a panic. During the swim, he'd lost his glasses and now he was almost blind. Joe and his gang took off, while I led Frannie into a residential neighborhood, where the two of us spent that night in the cemetery. Our clothes were soaking wet and we were freezing cold. The only comfort we had were the blankets we'd stored there years before. We were now exhausted. The only thing we could do was sleep.

The next morning, I left Frannie there and went out to steal food. The business of stealing is hard enough, but when the police are actively searching for you, it is damn near impossible. I could see the shopkeepers watching me and knew that something just wasn't right. I sprinted back to the cemetery to hide in the one place I knew as home, but it was too late. The police now knew our hiding-out spot. We were arrested within the hour. We'd been free from St. Aiden's for less than 74 hours.

Frannie and I were taken to the bridewell of the main police station in Liverpool, where we were questioned about the burglary. The police demanded that we give them the names of the others in the gang but we refused and remained tight-lipped. The next day, we appeared in front of a magistrate, charged with burglary and sent to Risley Remand Centre, just outside Warrington.

Risley was known by all who went there as "Grisley." It was famous for the many boys who attempted suicide while there and for the few who actually finished the job. The prison officer who booked me in mentioned that I was the youngest prisoner they currently had in the place. The courts ordered psychiatric evaluations of both Frannie and me, but due to the massive number of prisoners, those evaluations were never completed.

Risley housed some of the most notorious prisoners in the north of England. Child-killers, bank robbers, rapists and murderers made up the majority of the clientele. The British newspapers described it as a "sadistic, brutal, concentration camp." Former prisoners have attested to the fact that being interned there led to their lives spiraling out of control and into violence and addiction because of the trauma they endured at Risley.

We were locked up in single cells for twenty-three hours a day. The windows were a massive, square grid of steel framing, filled in with tiny square panes of glass. Every one of the glass panes had been smashed in my cell, so the place was absolutely freezing. The whole place stank with a mixture of body odor, excrement and pine disinfectant. It was as depressing as it could ever have been. The one saving grace of the whole ordeal was that Frannie was taken from there to the hospital to have his glasses replaced. During our one hour of time on the exercise yard that day, I'd never seen him as happy.

After two weeks at Risley, Frannie was sent once again to the Red Bank Secure Unit. The courts considered him far too unhinged to be around the average young thugs in the approved schools. I was sent to Foston Hall in the countryside of Derbyshire, for what the British government described as a short, sharp, shock.

CHAPTER 8
THE MOST PUNISHED CHILD IN BRITAIN

I was transported to Foston Hall in, again, a Black Mariah police vehicle, accompanied by four prison officers. One of the officers was in possession of my file. He must've been reading it on the journey because, during two hours of being thrown around by the van's crappy suspension on the winding, dirt roads of the Derbyshire countryside, I heard him refer to me as "the most punished child in Britain." Joe Kavanaugh and his gang, though, were never arrested for their part in the heist, yet their lives weren't any better than ours. The rest of the crew all died prematurely in horrific circumstances. Joe is the only one of his gang still living, as of this writing.

I was pulled out of the Black Mariah by the plain-clothed prison guards who'd been assigned to me. They maintained their vice-like grip on my arms during the short walk from the court-yard to the reception area. It was a strange and foreboding place, reminiscent of a prisoner-of-war camp; a Jacobean red-brick building, surrounded by a series of seemingly temporary prefabricated huts, most of which were arbitrarily spaced around the vast grounds of the camp. A tall wire fence topped with concertina razor wire surrounded the grounds, making it almost impossible to escape.

I should've been terrified at the sight of the place but I was numb. It was a numbness that penetrated deep inside my being. I was taken into a cold, stark reception area and given a uniform: a blue cotton shirt, gray trousers, and a pair of heavy, black boots. There was no mercy here and the men in charge were not typical teachers. They were military men; hard, chiseled, and fit as hell. They were supposed to be there to teach us to be men, and strong men at that, but just like in the approved schools, many of them had their own dirty, sinister agendas.

They screamed at me in the style of a drill sergeant.

"We'll make a man of you," they shouted and marched me frantically through the courtyard and into the dormitory.

There were many just like it. The dormitories were huts containing eight identical beds, lockers, and a "recess," a bathroom with sinks, showers, toilet cubicles without doors, and a long, trough-style urinal for the boys to piss in. This would be my life for the foreseeable future.

The daily routine is simple to explain but tough to deal with. We were made to wake up at six o'clock in the morning. We would shower, change into our uniforms, and make our beds to military standards. At six-thirty, we'd have inspection. We were then marched down to the external parade square and forced to march for one hour in our boots.

"Left, left, left, right, left…" screamed the teacher.

Breakfast was served in the dining hall at seven-thirty. We were given a bowl of porridge, a slice of toast, and a cup of tea. I was told by a kitchen worker that the tea contained a substance to stop us getting erections and ejaculating. God knows if that was true or not.

At just after eight, we were taken to the workhouse and given our work assignments. Most of the time, we sanded down steel engineering components. We'd dip the sandpaper in water and rub it along the components. It was a tiring job. After a few days, the skin began to fall from my hands.

At midday, we were taken to the dining hall for lunch. An average lunch consisted of roast potatoes and one other vegetable. Dessert would usually be yellow custard. After lunch, we'd be given one hour to relax on our beds before returning to the merciless sanding at 2 pm. The work would finish at four and we'd then be given two hours of marching and military calisthenics.

At just after 6 pm, we'd be served dinner. A typical dinner would consist of corned beef hash and cabbage. The food was basic but it did the job of filling our bellies. After dinner, we'd be made to shower, then it was back to the dormitory. There was no music or television for entertainment in the evenings. The only form of entertainment permitted was to sit and read in silence. Not me, though. I would lay on my bed and look at the stars out of the window on the opposite wall. They made me feel so small in the grand scheme of things and somehow the stars comforted my soul. I'd sometimes stare out of the window all night. The Hyper Vigilance caused by the years of abuse I'd suffered made it almost impossible to sleep soundly.

Every second day, instead of marching, we'd be made to do circuit training. The courtyard would be set up with weights, benches and racks. We'd be made to bench-press, do squats, shoulder presses, and arm curls. Between each station, we'd be ordered to complete twenty-five push-ups. There were three boards on the wall. The green board represented six reps, the red board represented eight reps, and the black board represented ten reps. Each boy would be classified by the color of their achievements. I made sure I was in the black category.

We began creating camaraderie through alliances. There were only two groups: the lads from Manchester and the lads from Liverpool. We stuck to our groups like glue and did what we could to out-perform our rivals. One day, a Manchester gangster confronted me. He told me he wanted a "straightener," a knock-down brawl to see who the alpha really was. He was bigger and tougher than me. Just like the multitude of brawls I'd had before, this was just another tree to chop down, as far as I was concerned, just another obstacle on a road full of them. I couldn't back down so I followed him out. I didn't wait. I head-butted him immediately, and before he had a chance to react, I rained down on him a massive onslaught of combinations.

I punched him repeatedly and didn't stop until one of the guards pulled me off him. I was taken to the governor and my punishment was to be confined to the isolation wing for fourteen days. It was a dormitory just like the others but I was the only inmate. I was kept in my pajamas and made to sit there alone. I was given 30 minutes a day to shower and one hour a day to exercise alone.

After my isolation, I was released back into the general population, and the regimen of work, training and sleeping continued. I could feel my spirit coming to life again and began to enjoy the training. I knew some of the meek lads were being abused by the guards, but some of us were becoming physically and mentally strong. The guards didn't realize the mistake they were making. They were breeding monsters.

I accepted my fate. I couldn't escape, but after four months, I was informed I was being released. My elation was short-lived. I was informed on the same day that I was to appear in front of another Magistrate's Court, where I'd probably be recommitted for another three years to a senior approved school. The torture was endless and unforgiving. Another three years, to a boy of 15, who'd spent a good percentage of his life in those hellish institutions of cruelty and mental torture, seemed like an eternity. I was genuinely sick to my stomach.

CHAPTER 9
THE DEVIL'S PLAYGROUND

Things happened exactly as they said. I was remanded to Risley Detention Centre for one night and then escorted to St. Joseph's Approved School in Nantwich, Cheshire. It looked like a country castle and was as forbidding on the inside as it was on the outside. It was run by the Christian Brothers, an order now known for its sadistic and sexually brutal treatment of children.

On the first day of my internment at St. Joseph's, I was cornered by a crew of Manchester thugs. They kicked the living shit out of me. I got a few punches in but there were just too many of them to deal with. I was left on the floor in a bloody mess. My life was on the line. Foston was inescapable, but this place didn't have a fence topped by barbed wire. As I was being carried on a stretcher into the ambulance, my mind was solely focused on escape.

The doctor in Crewe Infirmary's casualty department examined me, while a nurse stood behind him making notes on a clipboard. He gently pressed my nose and shook his head. He turned to the nurse and spoke to her in a whisper. She scratched down some more notes and nodded. He turned back to me and ran his hands down the side of my chest.

"Well, you don't have any broken ribs but that nose is broken."

He didn't need to tell me that. My eyes were black and so swollen that it was hard to see. I couldn't breathe through my nose and my head was swollen and pounding with pain.

The doctor and nurse left me for a few minutes to lie on the bed in the small cubicle. I was surrounded by a curtain, giving just a modicum of privacy. I could hear muffled voices and knew it wouldn't be long before I was back at that terrible place.

The curtain opened suddenly and a tall skinny man with black, greased-down hair, pale skin and an emotionless face walked into the cubicle. He stared down at me and flicked his head to the side.

"Get up and get your boots on," he said.

I did as he commanded and winced as I bent down to tie my shoelaces. It was obvious he was one of the Christian Brothers. You could tell he was a deviant prick, just by looking at him. He held the curtain open and flicked his head once more as a command for me to get out. We walked outside to a small car, where another brother was waiting for us in the driver's seat. I sat in the backseat by myself in total silence.

When we got back to St. Joseph's, I was placed in a room by myself. It was at the top of the main building, an attic room. It was creepy and the smell of the dust made it even more so. Ordinarily, the room would've unsettled me, but on this occasion, I was just content to be alone.

I didn't sleep well that night. My head was hurting and my nose was completely blocked. They left me alone most of the day and came to collect me for dinner. The same fella who'd taken me from the hospital slowly opened the door, and once again, stared down at me. He flicked his head at me and walked out of the room. I followed him down the stairs and into the dining hall.

I didn't want to eat. I was hungry but the pain of chewing was just too much to bear. I looked around the long wooden table. The lads were busy feeding their faces. The sound of the utensils clanking on the plates filled the room, but no-one said a word. If they had, there'd be hell to pay.

The next day, I was allowed in the yard. Some of the lads played football, some walked around the perimeter chatting. I just sat by myself on a wall next to the main building. I scanned my surroundings. There was only one brother keeping an eye on us and the wall around the perimeter wasn't that high, but it was high enough to conceal me if I chose to make a run for it. The perimeter gate would be an easy climb. I guessed I'd be over it with a single, swift jump.

I went for it. I waited for the brother to busy himself chastising a young boy for God knows what and I made a run for the gate. I bounced over it and landed in a full sprint away from the building. As I reached the main road, I saw a bus pulling up to a bus stop. I ran up its boarding steps and sank down onto a seat at the back. I had no money, so when the bus conductor got to me, I gave him my name and address and told him my mum would pay for the fare when we arrived in Crewe. I walked from the bus to the train station and boarded a train to Liverpool. I hid in the toilet all the way to avoid the ticket inspector.

At the Liverpool train station, I ran past the ticket collector at the gate. I kept running, and when I thought I was far enough from the train station, I found a bus stop and caught a bus to my mother's house on Scotland Road. Once again, I gave the bus conductor a false name and address.

I banged on the door of my mother's flat, and after a few minutes of waiting, she opened the door for me. She looked tired and distressed. She led me into the kitchen, sat me down at the small table, and made me some tea and a sandwich. She sat with me and gently touched my face to inspect the damage caused by the recent beating. She tried to hide it but I knew she was upset.

"You can't stay here, Terry," she said softly. "This is the first place they'll come to find you."

I felt my stomach churn. "I can't go back there, Mum," I pleaded.

I left the flat and walked to the end of the street. I'd fallen out with my old friend, David Hook, but I had nowhere else to turn so I knocked on his door. His mum answered, and within a few seconds, he came outside to talk to me. I asked if I could sleep in the shed at the back of his house and he agreed. He went back inside to fetch a blanket for me and then led me to the small brick building in the back garden.

It was freezing cold that night. There I was, on the floor, surrounded by gardening tools. Rain began pouring through the roof and I had to push myself into a corner to stop from being drenched.

I woke shivering the next morning. I lay still for a while, wrapped in the wet blanket and tensing every muscle in my body in an attempt to stop shivering. Before long, David's sister arrived at the shed with a cup of tea and a bacon and egg sandwich. I grabbed the cup of tea and held it close to me to warm me up. The tea and food comforted me, and when David's sister left, I lay down again and rested for a while.

My next visitor was David. I don't know where he got the money but he gave me a few pounds to see me through the day, so I took the bus to the City Centre. I walked the streets aimlessly, trying to think of my next move. It didn't take long for me to figure out what I was going to do. I happened to glance into the window of a parked car, a Morris 1100. The keys were right there in the ignition. I couldn't resist the impulse so I opened the unlocked door and drove through the city.

I was enjoying the experience for a while, until I spotted a motorcycle cop right behind me. He maintained his position. I tried to stay calm but I could feel the panic building inside me. I began to lose control of the car and I crashed it into a wall on Dock Road. I tried pulling at the car door but the pain in my leg drained me of the will to escape. The cop pulled open the door and dragged me violently out, unaware I'd broken my leg.

When he realized how hurt I was, he radioed for an ambulance and I was transported to the Liverpool Royal Infirmary, where I was admitted for the next ten days. They operated on my leg and placed it in a cast. On the tenth day, I was visited by the same Christian Brother who'd collected me from the hospital before. My heart sank when I realized I'd soon be back at St. Joseph's.

I was kept in solitary confinement for the next month. Food and books were brought to me but I only had one visitor, the headmaster, who informed me that the Crown Prosecution Service had placed the charges for car theft on hold.

After another week, I was once again transported to the infirmary and my cast was removed. My leg was still tender and it hurt to walk, so I was given a fiberglass brace for support. I was still kept in isolation and transported to Crewe Infirmary regularly for physiotherapy. All the while, my nose was still throbbing due to the beating I'd received on my first day in that hell-hole. The isolation was taking its toll on me. The whole experience was miserable.

Finally, I was released back into the system. I was placed in Brother McCarthy's class. He was old and thin, with gray, wispy hair and his face drawn in like a skeleton. He wore a black cassock and ran his class with an iron fist.

He would command each boy, one by one, to sit on his knee and read to the class while he held a book in front of their face. Eventually, it was my turn. As I was reading from the book he held, he slowly placed his free hand down the front of my trousers and tried to touch my genitals. I pulled away from him but he grabbed me by the scruff of my neck and tried to hold me in place. I yelled out and told him to get his hands off me. He released me and ordered me back to my desk, but I just knew I was in for some trouble.

When he finally dismissed the class, he told me to stay seated. He waited for the room to be empty and then grabbed me by the neck and screamed at me to do as I was told. He then punched me as hard as he could on the jaw before ordering me out of his classroom.

The next day, my face was swollen like a melon. I was distraught and finally mustered up the courage to go to the headmaster's office. The old man sat there and listened to my complaints about McCarthy.

"Tell him to leave me alone and stop hitting me," I demanded as I held back tears.

The headmaster dismissed me. I knew my words had fallen on deaf ears. That same day, I was approached by the Manchester gang who'd kicked my head in on my first day. They wanted another fight. I told them I'd see them again when my leg was healed. I had no friends at St. Joseph's. All the other lads were from Manchester or Cheshire.

Eventually, I was allowed to spend most of my time in the welding workshop, for an hour in the morning and an hour in the afternoon. Throughout that whole six months, I had no formal education.

I waited out my time, and one day, I was told my sentence at St. Joseph's was over. Relief came over me like a soft wind. I began to mentally prepare for the outside world and fantasized about where I would go and what I would do.

I was in the welding workshop one day and one of the brothers approached me and told me to go to the headmaster's office. As I walked in, I was met by two men sitting on the sofa in his office. They wore suits and ties and instantly I knew they were detectives.

They stood and told me to put my hands behind my back. I did as I was told and they placed me in handcuffs. I was transported to the Magistrate's Court and led through the side door of the ominous, Hanoverian building. The guards placed me in a cell, uncuffed my hands, and gave me a lunch of a ham sandwich and a glass of milk.

When released from St. Joseph's, I was arrested for some old charges of theft, which were brought forward. That meant I would be sent to Borstal, the place we all dreaded the most.

I waited for what seemed like hours before I was escorted to appear before the magistrate. He read the charges against me and then ordered that I be placed in custody, on remand, until my sentencing at Liverpool Crown Court. He looked over his golden, half-moon framed glasses and informed me that I should be sentenced to between six months and two years at a Borstal. The impact of his words shot through me like a bullet.

Once again, I was transported to "Grisley" Risley Remand Centre. It was now June and my court date was in September, so I knew I had to stay there for a minimum of three months. Just days after I arrived, a riot was started, led by a group of older prisoners, headed up by the infamous Eddie Davis. They climbed the roof in protest, so the prison officers locked down all the prisoners for twenty-four hours a day. We were allowed only one meal a day.

The conditions were terrible. The rioters set fire to the roof and the whole place was mayhem. There was no rest and the noise was constant all throughout the night. Sleep was impossible.

As the weeks drew on, things began to settle down. I was in the same wing of the building as the other youths who were heading off to Borstal. We began chatting and grew quite close. One of the lads, Tommy Mills, was from Liverpool, and although we had never met, we had mutual friends. We tried to stay away from the subject of the Borstal system. It was too much for us to take, given the circumstances. We all knew those institutions were infamous for violence and severe sexual assaults. We'd all heard the horror stories and didn't need reminding.

Eventually, six of us were transported to the magnificent Liverpool Crown Court and placed in the stone cells underneath the building. There were two of us in each cell. I was placed with Tommy. We were left alone, and within a few minutes, Tommy began to shake. He broke down and told me he didn't think he would be able to survive being in a Borstal. I tried to calm him down but he was beginning to infect me with his fear. I was unnerved. After all, this was the first time I'd seen anyone exhibit real and absolute fear.

When the guards came for me, it was a relief to be away from Tommy. I climbed the stairs and stood in the dock. It felt like I was climbing onto a gallows. The judge was Judge Wickham. I'd heard of him before. He was known as "Wicked Wickham" because of his complete lack of compassion.

He sat there in his red robe, adorned with a purple sash and a long, white wig, and without so much as looking up at me, sentenced me to between six months and two years of "Borstal training." He was done with me in less than a minute and the guards then ordered me back to the cell. When Tommy saw me, he rushed towards me, scrambling for answers or clues of what his own fate might be. The guards grabbed him and he was next.

When he returned to the cell, he was sobbing uncontrollably. I tried to console him but my words had no impact. I watched him crying on the floor in a fetal position and it dawned on me that I was barely sixteen and I'd already been sentenced to eleven-and-a-half years in various God-forsaken institutions.

That evening, the six of us were handcuffed, placed on a bus, and transported to Strangeways Prison in Manchester. We arrived at 7 pm. This was the first time I'd been in a real prison. We were led to a special wing on the second floor. This was where Borstal boys were prepped. We were fed and placed in individual cells, isolated from each other. This was unlike the approved schools where I could easily escape. Tommy was in the cell next to mine. I knew he was in trouble mentally. But there was nothing I could do. All I could manage was to wait.

I was woken up at 7 am by the sound of a guard unlocking my cell. I glanced out of the door and noticed that the cell next to mine was covered in plastic sheeting. I asked the guard what the plastic was for but he didn't answer me.

After a week in that cell, we were once again made to board a bus. This time, there were only five of us. Tommy had hanged himself in the cell next to mine. Our next stop was Everthorpe Borstal in Hull. The journey was silent and the air in the bus was thick with fear.

CHAPTER 10
BORSTAL: A SHORT, SHARP, SHOCK

As soon as we entered the long, paved drive, the heads of the lads began to turn. We'd arrived on the estate and now it was only a matter of minutes before we made it to our final destination, Everthorpe Borstal, Hull.

The estate had once been the home of an affluent family and was nestled in an undulating green landscape that covered a distance as far as the eye could see on both sides. It was one of the many beautiful landscapes Yorkshire was known for. The manor house was still there and looked like a castle, complete with parapets and flanked by giant stone lions.

It wasn't long before we arrived at the gates that were the only entry through the massive stone walls that surrounded the facility. When the gates slowly opened and the bus made its way inside, my heart sank. This was obviously a prison and a seemingly inescapable one at that. I knew right then and there that this would be tougher than I originally thought.

The doors of the bus opened and a prison officer in a uniform resembling a copper's climbed onto the stairs of the bus screaming, "Let's be 'avin you. Get off the bus!"

We all scrambled from our seats and barreled down the narrow aisle, pushing and pulling one another in an attempt to get off the bus first. We were yelled at to get into three ranks. Those of us who had survived the approved schools knew exactly what that meant and did as we were told, but those who hadn't were grabbed by any available body part by one of the many prison officers, whom we referred to as 'screws,' and were forced into the ranks.

The screw who had unceremoniously forced us off the bus, Mr. Rogers, began to scream more orders at us, but I couldn't hear a word he was saying. All I could do was retreat into my own mind and block out any thoughts I had at that moment. I was not afraid. I was completely numb.

The Borstal system had been created at the end of the nineteenth century by The Gladstone Committee and was an attempt to separate youths from the older convicts. Its name was a homage to the first such institution, which was established in the village of Borstal in Kent. The intent of The Gladstone Commission had been to expose young offenders to a system of education instead of punitive justice, while instilling a military-style discipline. The road to Hell is paved with good intentions and this place was no different.

I tried to keep my head still but couldn't resist looking around. This horrendous place was built with four wings of merciless-looking stone and brick, with each wing named after each of the four British patron saints. I was to be housed in St. George's wing.

Rogers' speech came to a halt. We were ordered to turn right with the command, "Right turn!"

Some of the lads stayed still, frozen in place, some turned left. Those boys were screamed at and pulled in the right direction. I was one of the lads who moved correctly without thought. Again, I knew this would be tough but my life had been filled with institutions for a long time, and if anyone could survive, or even thrive in this place, it was me.

We were marched into a reception area, where we were stripped down to our underwear and hurriedly given a gray uniform to wear. Basic necessities were pushed into our hands or thrown at us: bedding, boots, and clothing that filled our arms. From there, we were marched into the main housing wing. It was two floors of dorms. The staircase and upper walkways were steel and the walls were white-washed brick. The ground floor was packed with plain, bolted-down tables and steel folding chairs for the lads, as a dining area. Some of the inmates watched us from the upper walkways as we entered. They leaned over the wall and smirked as we caught their eyes.

We were all marched into the dorm, and as the door opened, we were told to step inside and be assigned a bunk. The place didn't seem so bad. It had all the necessary furniture: beds, desks, and lockers.

The regimen was militaristic. A screw would bang on the door at exactly 6 am, and by 6.30 am, we had to be washed and ready for the day. We were each assigned a job. I was placed on cleaning duty and would clean all the common areas. I didn't mind it, really. For the most part, I was left alone to scrub the floors on my knees, mop the floors, and clean the toilets. The first couple of days weren't so bad.

We were made to march in the mornings and evenings, a practice that was supposed to foster an attitude of teamwork. We'd have an hour of physical fitness a day, and if a boy could prove himself to be worthy, he'd eventually be taught a trade, such as carpentry or welding. That wasn't even close to being on the cards for me at that time but I lived in hope.

I kept my head down and tried to avoid conflict. I'd seen some of the vicious fights that occurred and was amazed I'd kept clear of that nonsense. The weak, frail-looking lads got the worst of it. When we'd all sit at the tables on the ground floor for our meals, they'd be made to hand over their food to the bullies. Some of the kids would be routinely, viciously beaten, and more often than not, they'd be raped.

On many occasions, the wing would be locked down after one of the lads would smash a window in the dorm and cut his wrists or neck with the glass. For those poor souls, death was a far better option than to live in their miserable environment. I'll never forget the haunting sound of the ambulance sirens getting louder as they approached.

One day, I was approached by a Scottish lad, who told me "The Daddy" wanted to see me upstairs in the recess, the place where the lads would shower and brush their teeth. I knew what that meant. The Daddy was the toughest lad on the wing, who unofficially called the shots. Usually, he would prove himself to earn that position by scrapping with anyone he thought might undermine him. That day, it was my turn. The Daddy on my wing was a massive black lad called Redhead. I was nervous but I tried not to show it. I nodded at the lad who'd brought me the message and he left in a hurry.

I found two Liverpool lads and asked them to back me up. They agreed and we made our way up the stairs to the recess bathroom. My heart was pounding. With each step, I willed myself into a frenzy and could feel the adrenaline surging through my veins. Redhead was waiting for me, leaning up against a sink. He pushed himself off to approach me, and without hesitation, I ran at him, grabbed him by the ears and gave him the infamous "Liverpool kiss," a head-butt right on the bridge of his nose. It landed with perfect precision. He fell to the floor like a sack of spuds and I began to stomp on him. My boots landed down hard on his head, torso and limbs. Any and all available targets got stomped on with all my might.

The melee must have alerted the screws, because within seconds, the Liverpool lads had bolted off and the sounds of police whistles filled the stale air. Out of nowhere, four screws appeared and grabbed me. Each one took a limb and carried me vertically down the stairs and out to a small building next to the main wing. I was thrown into a small cell with nothing more than a mattress and a Bible, and left there all night.

The next morning, the door opened and I was marched by Rogers and another screw to the Governor's office. The Governor was an old, thin man, with wispy gray hair and gold-rimmed glasses. Without any emotion, he looked up at me and asked me to explain myself. I told him that Redhead and I had had a straightener, pure and simple. I told him the truth without any embellishments but knew I'd be in for some severe punishment.

He gave me 21 days of solitary confinement. I was taken back to the cell I'd spent the previous night in and left there. For the duration of my time in that cell, my meals would be brought to me, I was taken to the recess to wash, and I was allowed one hour to walk around the building by myself in the evening. For a 16-year-old, being separated and walled up like a rabid animal, was absolute torture.

As soon as I was taken back to the dorm, life changed for me. Now I was The Daddy. I had no desire to be a tyrant, though. In essence, things just got more peaceful for me. The weaker lads would often ask me to intervene when they were being bullied and I did that with pleasure, relishing watching the bullies cower when I'd approach them. After my straightener with Redhead, I never had to fight again in Everthorpe because my reputation preceded me.

I kept my nose clean, and after a while, I was transferred from cleaning duties to the woodwork shop and thoroughly enjoyed it. At last, I was actually learning something and the teachers seemed passionate about teaching what they knew. I served a total of ten months in Everthorpe.

The Borstal system was so brutal that the Thatcher government of the 1980s had to shut it down, since report after report of the horrors perpetrated in those institutions became public knowledge. To this day, the Borstal system is a stain on the history of the British judiciary.

CHAPTER 11
SNATCHES AND NIGHT SAFES

I left Borstal with absolutely nothing, but the system made me stronger, both mentally and physically. You can't survive that system unless you fortify yourself. Most of the other lads were broken, mentally destroyed, but not me.

I arrived back in Liverpool and contacted two of the old gang, Ronnie Gibbons and John James. The last time I'd seen them, we were kids. Now we were men. They'd grown into beasts. They were both skilled boxers and trained like madmen. Now all we needed was a plan. Before long, we'd hatched a plot to do what we did best: robbery.

Mondays and Fridays were our chosen days to work. Each week, we'd target a supermarket. On Monday evenings, after closing, a manager would be sent to the local bank to deposit the weekend's intake of cash. On Fridays, the prior week's intake would be deposited. We'd follow a short distance behind, and just before he'd get to the bank, we'd pounce. We were far too quick for there to be any violence. Before he even knew what was happening, we'd grab the bag and be dodging through the back alleys. We did this for weeks and never got caught.

At this time, I found out that Mum had lung cancer. I tried to visit her as often as possible. Then the inevitable happened, when I was 16 years old. I lost my Mum to the disease. It was tough when she died. I just wanted to get away, so I went to stay with my older brother, John, in Brighton.

I had no money, so I began shoplifting. I was good at it. I'd steal food, clothes and other small items. Some of the loot I'd sell just to get through the day. One day, my luck changed. I was walking out of Debenhams department store with a bag containing two shirts that I'd stolen and I was confronted by two police officers. I dropped the bag and ran. I thought I was home free but they took fingerprints off the bag and that would come back to haunt me.

A few weeks later, I went back to Liverpool and met up with John James. He told me he'd been following a woman, who'd leave work on Friday afternoons, get the bus from Norris Drive to Queen's Drive, and walk to Barclay's bank, where she'd deposit money.

We waited for her, just past the bus stop on Queen's Drive. She was a middle-aged woman of slight build. She didn't even notice us. I grabbed her bag and we ran. We soon got to Liverpool City Centre and rifled through the bag. It contained £550, a small fortune. We bought clothes from Burton's, and when we were all dressed up, we went for a night out on the town. We ended up in The Hermitage, a well-known pub on Queen's Drive. At 9 pm, John left. I was talking to a guy at the bar, when two uniformed cops and two detectives walked in.

The uniformed sergeant walked right up to me and said, "Get outside!"

I panicked. The sergeant poked his truncheon into my stomach to intimidate me. I grabbed the stick and hit him in the face and neck with the pint glass full of lager I had in my hand. I tried to run, but one of the detectives pushed me and I went straight through the window. I landed outside in the parking lot. The cops followed and began raining kicks down on me that landed on my head, legs, back and stomach. All I could do was lay there helplessly in a fetal position.

My arm and two fingers were almost severed. I was taken to Walton General Hospital, where a team of surgeons performed emergency surgery on me. I woke up after the surgery to find myself handcuffed to a bed with a cop stationed outside the room.

Two days after the surgery, I was visited by the two detectives, who informed me they were taking me back to Brighton and that I was being charged with the theft of the two shirts I'd stolen. They were also charging me with the assault on the police officer.

A few days later, I was escorted to Brighton, and after being charged, I was placed on remand in Lewis Prison.

I was given a bed on the hospital wing, where they monitored my arm. The flesh was cut to the bone. I received 283 stitches and extensive nerve damage and was told I needed physiotherapy. One of the inmates took care of me. He'd bring me my meals and chat to me to alleviate the boredom. It wasn't long before I found out that he was Gordon Goody, one of the Great Train Robbers! I told him everything about myself. He made a point at times to quietly listen. Just talking to him was therapy.

I waited in the prison for two months for the Crown Court in Brighton, which gave me a two-year sentence. I was sent to Wormwood Scrubs in London as a young prisoner. I knew I'd be in for a hard time but I never imagined the place would be as brutal as it was.

My cell mate, Johnny, was from Scotland. We connected instantly. When you're in prison, things get territorial and everyone who thinks they're hard enough tries to take control. Even the most trivial things on the outside can be life and death when you're inside.

Two black guys had taken over the ping-pong table. They played constantly, and even when they weren't playing, they'd sit right next to the table, preventing anyone from getting anywhere near it. Johnny and I decided their days of annexing the ping-pong game were over. Within the first week, we waited for them to go and get their meals. After they'd left, we broke the wooden legs off a chair. When they went back to their cell to eat, we followed them and beat them senseless with the chair legs. Finished, we quietly walked out of their cell and locked the door.

It wasn't long before we were being dragged from our cell by a team of screws. We were both punished with a month of solitary confinement. I was locked in a cell for 23 hours a day, with nothing but a mattress and a Bible. I was allowed to walk inside the solitary block for one hour by myself.

In the first week, I was visited by the Governor. I asked him if I could be moved to Liverpool to be closer to my family. Two weeks later, I got good news; I was being moved to Her Majesty's Prison Walton in Liverpool.

When I arrived at HMP Walton, many of the lads I'd served time with in Borstal were there. I was greeted like a rock star. The lads came out in droves to see me. They shared their soap and toothpaste with me and made sure I was comfortable.

I was given a job folding shirts in the laundry. I was still nursing my injured arm, so they made sure I was given light duties. I was told I could use the gym for physiotherapy and it was there that I met the notorious Paul Sykes. He was big, with a handle-bar mustache and a face that'd seen many violent encounters. He was a renowned heavy-weight boxer and could bench press 450 lbs. He had a reputation of being crazy but he was a friendly guy; to me, anyway.

The prison was filled with some of Britain's most violent, Category A gangsters. Norman Johnson was one of them. He was a gangster from Liverpool, who admitted to organizing a plot to kill the Kray Twins. He told me he'd met me in Wormwood Scrubs. In Walton, he took me under his wing and looked out for me.

The screws were generally decent men but there was always one who'd take a dislike to someone. The one who took a dislike to me was Thompson. In the mornings, he wouldn't open my cell. He did this for days, and one day, I just flipped. I told him that I was going to "do him." He didn't care, and the next morning, he did it again. When he eventually opened the door, I threw my piss pot at him and it hit him on the head, knocking him senseless. Six of the screws rushed me and carried me out of the cell. I was once again taken to the block, spent 28 days in solitary confinement and lost two weeks of remission.

I spent 16 months in Walton and was released in March, 1975, with the two shirts I had stolen from Debenhams. I laughed at the irony. I decided to wear the yellow Ben Sherman shirt for the walk down Hormby Road and through Walton Park. The rain was pouring down and it soaked me to the skin. As I walked, I realized that my mother wouldn't be there to greet me.

I arrived at the house and my father was there. He looked old and frail. I knew his heart had been bothering him and that he'd even attempted suicide on more than one occasion. I was relieved to be out in the free world, but the sight of him depressed me. He made me a cup of tea and told me my older brother, Alan, was on the way to meet us. Alan was four years older than me and I respected him.

When he eventually arrived, he told me he had a plan to take me to Southampton, where he'd get me a job on the world's most legendary and luxurious cruise liner, The Queen Elizabeth II, the most famous cruise ship in the world, which everyone called The QEII. Alan had worked on her for years and had been on the ship for its maiden voyage in 1969. I'd heard his stories and was anxious to see the ship first-hand.

CHAPTER 12
ANNETTE AND ELIZABETH

A few days before I boarded the QEII for its world cruise, Alan and I went to a nightclub, the Knightsbridge. It was jammed with young people having a great deal of fun. While we were standing at the bar, I noticed a really great-looking woman, who was with a friend. My instant thought was, She is the one! I asked her to dance. She agreed.

"What's your name?" I said.

"Annette."

We danced for a long time, during which I told her I was going away for four months.

"Would you wait for me, Annette?"

"Yes, I will," she said.

During the time I was away, I wrote to her and we spoke a few times on the phone. After I came home, we dated, and after six months, I asked her to marry me. Our wedding was held at the Huyton Suite in Liverpool, with 400 guests. We went to London and Brighton on our honeymoon. Annette was one of the loveliest women I had ever met. In the future, she would share her life and work together with me several times in America, including when I was a butler, and when we went to Hawaii. In 1989, Annette would give birth to our daughter, Kelly.

But life was not always a bed of roses. Annette suffered from breast cancer, due, I am convinced, to the pressures we were often under. But, thankfully, she overcame the disease. Because of this and other issues, as well as my own that continued to haunt me from childhood, we would decide to divorce in 2004, but we have remained the best of friends, especially for Kelly's sake.

All too soon, a short while after I met Annette, it was time for me to take the job on the QEII. I stayed at my father's house for just over a week until the day Alan came to collect me. We drove from Liverpool to Southampton, and on the way, he clued me in on his plan for me. His friend, Harry Duffy, had worked for Cunard Line Shipping Company for decades and had contacts who could get me a job.

Harry was there to greet us when we arrived at his flat. He was a short guy with thinning hair and a pot belly. He greeted us like old friends and had set up his spare room for Alan and me. He said he'd arranged an interview for me at Cunard as a Specialist Cook. The interview wasn't until the week after we arrived, so in the evenings preceding, the three of us would go off to the local pub to drink.

I'd sit there and watch Alan and Harry drink all evening. I'd never been that interested in heavy drinking, so I spent the evenings watching them get absolutely pie-eyed drunk. It was evident that Harry was an alcoholic.

Eventually, I arrived at the Cunard building on the Southampton Docks. The guy who interviewed me was pleasant enough, but it was evident that Harry had spun him a story about me being a trained and somewhat experienced chef. I was given my papers, and the next day, I was boarding the ship.

I'd never seen anything like it. It was 963 feet long and weighed over 70,000 tons. The world's elites traveled from Southampton to New York on the ship regularly and now I'd be working on it for the foreseeable future. Harry led me to the Purser's office, where I was given my papers and he then left me alone to my new life as a chef.

I was shown my living quarters, a small cabin shared with two others in the center of the ship. It wasn't anything special but it beat my former accommodations in prison.

My new career began the morning after I arrived. We were up at 5 am, and by 5.30 am, we were hard at work. Seasickness was a problem for me and quite a few of the other lads. There was the constant smell of vomit below deck. Eventually, I became accustomed to the motion of the ship and my seasickness wasn't too bad.

The head chef gave me a corner of the kitchen to chop vegetables. It was evident at the outset that I had no idea what I was doing. As luck would have it, there was another Liverpool lad working as a chef in the kitchen. His name was Tony Lawless. He took to me instantly and took me under his wing, teaching me everything there was to know about preparing vegetables.

After work, we'd go to the staff bar for drinks. It was known as The Pig. The designers of the ship had made it to resemble a comfortable, local pub. I wasn't much of a drinker, but I'd go there for a few pints in the evening, just to be sociable. Many of the staff were from the North of Ireland. We'd often sit together and chat the night away.

Five days into the voyage, we arrived in New York. As we came into port, I marveled at the skyline and the sight of The Statue of Liberty. Tony and I walked through the city. We took 42nd street and had lunch in Times Square. The whole place looked decrepit but I loved it. We went shopping for clothes and everything seemed so inexpensive. I'd been told that my old friend, Ronnie Gibbons, was training out of a gym somewhere in New York. I hadn't seen him since he was in my gang as a young child and I really wanted to connect with him, but we didn't have time. We had to be back on the ship at six 6 pm to start work.

When we returned to Southampton, Tony took the train to Liverpool and I stayed with Harry in Southampton. I asked Alan if he knew where Ronnie was training, and within a few hours, he got all the information I needed.

A few days later, I was back on the ship for another five-day cruise to New York. When we docked in New York, I took a taxi to Gleason's Gym in Manhattan. I was greeted there by Gil Clancy, a famous trainer to some of the best boxers in the world. Within twenty minutes, Ronnie walked in with his gym bag slung over his shoulder. He was tall and lean, with a little bit of soft tissue damage to his face.

I watched him training: jumping rope, bag work, shadow

boxing, and heavy sparring that covered the next four hours. When he was done, we headed off to Times Square for salad and a glass of water. We talked about old times and reminisced about being kids in the old neighborhood of Scotland Road. He told me that he was going to be the Welterweight Champion of the World and I told him how amazed I was that, after all we'd been through, we were sitting together, chatting it up in New York City. Before long, I was bidding him farewell and we arranged to meet again when I was next in New York.

I didn't like working in the kitchen and made that quite clear in The Pig on a few occasions. One day, one of the Irish lads told me there were jobs going as waiters and that I should apply. I did just that, and within a few days, I was transferred to the restaurants, private rooms and bars as a waiter. My uniform was a yellow fitted jacket, black tuxedo trousers, and a white shirt with a black bow-tie. The first week was a steep learning curve, when I was schooled in all aspects of serving society's elites.

I loved it and I loved it even more when I saw the tips I was making. I seemed to be a natural. The guests loved me, and before long, I was approached by one of the General Managers, who asked me to apply for the position of Butler in the penthouses. I applied, and within a few days, I was wearing the grey suit of one of the most lucrative and highly esteemed positions on the ship, The Butler.

The penthouse consisted of 16 luxurious suites and a restaurant known as The Queen's Grill. I was placed in the care of another Liverpool lad, who would teach me all the tricks of the trade. Pinky Purcell got his name from the fact that his face was bright pink in color. He had grey hair and was as rough as any working-class man from Liverpool, but he was fun and had a heart of gold. The guests and staff alike loved him. It was hard work and attention to detail was paramount, but it was rewarding and extremely enjoyable.

A few weeks into the job, Pinky pulled me aside and brought out the guest list for the upcoming journey from New York to

Southampton. Elizabeth Taylor and Richard Burton would be our guests. On a Thursday afternoon, as the guests were boarding, Pinky and I were waiting next to the door of the penthouse lift. When it opened, the movie-star couple stepped out to meet us. Elizabeth was glowing. She was dressed in an all-black dress, which hugged her frame to reveal her near-perfect body. They were so gracious. She introduced herself to me and Richard just nodded.

We had already hung up their clothes and prepared the room, so we asked them if we could make them a drink. They agreed and then we left them alone in the room. Each evening, they'd dine in the Queen's Grill, where a personal chef would prepare such favorites as caviar and filet mignon. While they were eating, Pinky and I would service their room. We'd change the towels, turn down the bed and leave a rose and chocolates on the pillows.

The couple arrived back early one day, while I was still servicing the room. Richard went out to the balcony to smoke a cigar and Elizabeth began talking to me.

"Have you ever thought about being a movie star, Terry?" she asked.

"No, ma'am, I haven't. I don't think that life would suit me," I replied.

She had no idea who I really was and didn't know about my criminal past.

She shrugged. "Well, you should at least be a butler in California. They'd love you there and I'm sure you'd love Santa Monica. It's so pretty."

As she was talking, she was taking off her diamond necklace and placing it in the top drawer of the dresser in the room. She then took off her diamond earrings and placed them in the same drawer. I covertly glanced inside and saw that it was stacked to the brim with jewelry.

CHAPTER 13
A ROYAL HEIST

I arrived at The Pig one evening and my eyes were drawn straight to the bar. Seated on a stool, all alone, was one of the most beautiful women I'd ever seen. She was slim, with curves in all the right places. Her straight, black hair fell down her back, almost touching her seat. I just had to introduce myself. I approached her.

"Hello. Do you mind if I sit here?" I asked.

"Not at all," she responded in the most wonderful, bubbly, East London accent.

Her name was Anna. She was only nineteen years old, but she was the general manager of the ship's jewelry shop. By the end of the evening, she had agreed to go to dinner with me when we docked in New York on our next voyage and we were on the fast track to becoming good friends.

We would meet regularly in the evenings for a drink after her shift. One day, she told me she wouldn't be able to meet me because she had to take a stock inventory of the shop and that she'd have to work into the evening. I asked if I could keep her company while she worked and she obliged.

I'd never been in the jewelry shop before but it was evident as soon as I arrived that most of the jewelry was high-end. I tried to be as nonchalant as possible.

"How much do you think all the jewelry's worth?" I asked. I figured they were either Elizabeth Taylor's jewels or the shop's, in the display cases. It was a huge amount.

"Probably just over a million," she responded. "We'll be putting some display cases in here when we dock in Southampton. We'll be stocking them with over three-and-a-half million pounds' worth of jewelry."

What she said got the cogs in my mind turning. All I could think about for the rest of the journey home was the jewelry. I knew Ronnie Gibbons was just waiting for a chance at hitting the big time and I needed a good man to help me off-load the loot in New York. He would be ideal. When we arrived in Southampton, I stayed put in Harry's flat and plotted the job in my head. I paced the floor endlessly, thinking about every angle.

The next five-day journey to New York was crucial. I stopped by the jewelry shop many times on the pretext of visiting Anna, paying close attention to the new display cases. By the time we reached New York, I was ready to explain every facet of the job to Ronnie.

I took a taxi to the gym and watched Ronnie train, as I had before. Afterwards, we visited Times Square, where we partook of our customary salads. When we sat down to eat, I explained the plan to Ronnie. I told him we'd arrive at the jewelry shop early in the morning, wearing ski masks and gloves. We'd then smash the display cases with a fire extinguisher and quickly grab the jewelry. Ronnie would take the loot from me off the ship when we landed in New York and we'd split the profits. Ronnie's eyes shone and he nodded. I could see that he was in, 100 per cent. Ronnie was tough and feared no man. He wouldn't let me down. Eventually, I decided to persuade Ronnie not to steal Elizabeth Taylor's jewels. I liked her. Maybe I'd just go for the display cases instead.

I did take Ronnie onto the ship that evening and began showing him around. We were walking down one of the corridors and I could feel eyes on me. I turned to see two of the masters-at-arms following us, with two other men behind them. I was approached by the older one, whom I'd seen many times before.

"I know who you are, but who's he?" he said, pointing at Ronnie.

"He's a friend of mine. I'm showing him around the ship," I replied.

"He leaves now, and when he's gone, these fellas want a word with you,"

He pointed at the men behind him. Just by looking at them, I knew they were coppers. I walked Ronnie back to the gangplank.

"What do they want with you?" he whispered. I shrugged and bid him farewell.

As I walked back towards them, my stomach began to churn and my mind filled with questions. Am I going to be arrested? Has someone stitched me up for a crime I didn't commit? Did someone find out that we were planning a robbery?

The detectives were calm and polite enough. They told me they wanted to speak to me when we got back to Southampton and then left me alone to get back to my duties. When we arrived back in Southampton, I was instructed to go to the Cunard building, close to the docks. When I arrived, I was taken to a small office, where the two detectives were waiting for me. What they told me next chilled me to the bone. They informed me that the Irish Republican Army had infiltrated the ship and had gained employment as waiters and bartenders and had been foiled in a plan to destroy the ship with the plastic explosive called Semtex.

They said I'd been seen drinking with a few of the suspects and asked me if I was a member of the IRA. I told them over and over again that I had chatted and had drinks with them, but I had no idea who they really were. The coppers spent over two hours questioning me but seemed to believe me in the end.

I thought I was in the clear but then they told me they had performed a detailed background check on me and now knew about my past and my fraudulent application. I was informed that Cunard had banned me from the ship and that I could collect my last paycheck the next morning. Once again, I was back at square one. My only option was to return to Liverpool.

CHAPTER 14
THE QUEEN'S FORTUNE

I was 22 years old but I was in the same position I had been in when I was ten. I felt desperate. All I wanted to do was work, but with my criminal record, I knew no-one would want to employ me.

On a cold, Friday morning in December, I was standing at a bus stop when I was approached by an old friend of mine. Dave and I were in approved school together. He was short, with cropped, blond hair and he didn't fear anyone. He was from the notorious Huyton area of Liverpool and I knew he was involved with an organized group of bank robbers from that neighborhood. He knew of my reputation so he confided in me and told me he was on his way to plan a bank robbery in the town of Bootle. He asked me to join him.

We arrived at the Girobank Headquarters in Bootle approximately half an hour later. Dave's friend, Jacko, was waiting close by in a Ford Cortina. Jacko was 5ft. 2 in. tall, with dyed black hair. He was in his fifties and had a reputation as one of the best bank robbers in the north-west of England.

The Girobank was a giant steel and glass structure that dwarfed all the buildings nearby. It was surrounded by fields and trees that allowed us to watch all the activity, all the comings and goings, without being seen. It was the central location where money was transported to each post office in Liverpool. The money was used for the sole purpose of paying government benefits to those who needed them for such things as pensions, unemployment and child benefits. They were all delivered, usually, on Friday mornings and there was often a long queue of people waiting to receive them when the armored van arrived.

Dave drew my attention to an armored van that was leaving the building. He told me he'd followed each of them and that this one made approximately seven deliveries, with the first delivery to the post office in Cantril Farm and at Withens Post Office. Dave had made a guess that the van would leave the Girobank carrying approximately £50,000-£100,000. He tapped on his watch as the van drove by us. The time was exactly 9 am.

He informed me that the van would reach Withens at exactly 9:25 am , as it had done numerous times before. It would take him and Jacko a few months to plan the logistics, but when all the details were confirmed, the two of them would rob the van with a handgun and a sawn-off shotgun. They asked me to be the getaway driver. I told them I'd think about it.

A few weeks later, I met Dave and Jacko at Dave's house in Huyton. I told them I wasn't interested in their job but that I'd followed another van that had made nine stops, the first of which was at Moss Lane Post Office in Sefton, and that I wanted to pull off that job with my own team. We shook hands and went our separate ways.

Now I was excited. I contacted a member of the gang I formed when I was eight years old. John James was now tall, slim and fit, with black hair and piercing blue eyes. By just looking at him, anyone would've thought he was Superman. I told him my plan and he was all in with it.

I began planning the job, but in the meantime, we needed money and a means to test my methods, so we began on a smaller scale by robbing the compact-sized vans that were used to deliver smaller amounts of money.

We arrived at Henry Lane Post Office, Maghull, at exactly 9 am and waited in line. We'd followed this particular van for two weeks and knew it would be arriving soon. We wore hats, leather gloves and overcoats. I carried a claw hammer concealed in my coat. It was a weapon to be used as a last resort.

The van pulled up slowly. The driver was only about 5ft. 1in. tall and looked out of shape. He parked the van, walked to the rear doors, and popped them open, then pulled out a heavy, green canvas bag and heaved it over his shoulder. His escort exited the passenger side, carrying The Screamer, a black box with a button on it that would sound a deafening alarm if either of them were to get into trouble.

As the Postmaster unlocked the front doors of the Post Office and the driver walked towards the doors, I ran to the driver and grabbed the bag from the rear. The driver instantly let go of the bag and John and I ran. As we made our way through the back streets and alleyways, we could hear The Screamer getting softer in the distance. We had a stolen car staged about a half a mile away. I threw the bag in the boot of the car and we drove to a safehouse in Anfield.

We arrived at the beautiful red brick house a few minutes later. We parked behind it in a back alley and entered through the back door. The house was owned by my friend Rava, who greeted us and led us up the stairs and into a bedroom. I threw the bag onto the bed and noticed that the seal of the bag had the amount it contained stamped onto it. The bag contained £16,500. We were delighted. Rava stored the bag in his loft for us, where it would remain until it was needed.

The second job was even easier than the first. This time, I brought another friend with us. His name was Tommy Doherty. Tommy was 6ft. tall with wild, curly hair and teeth that looked like an old graveyard. His whole family were gangsters. He was crazy but trustworthy.

John was waiting next to a Post Office in a stolen car. Tommy and I joined the queue of people waiting outside. Again, we wore hats, gloves and heavy coats. I would be the guy who snatched the bag, Tommy would be my back-up, and John was the getaway driver.

As soon as the van arrived, the driver exited and walked slowly to the back of the van.

As he opened the door and grabbed the bag, I ran at him and shouted, "Give me the bag!"

Without a beat, the driver threw the bag at me and both Tommy and I ran to the car and jumped in. There was no noise from The Screamer this time. I suspected the driver and his escort were too shocked to activate it.

John sped off to Derby Village, where we'd staged a Bedford van in a church car park. We switched vehicles and drove to a flat in Cantril Farm, where another friend of mine greeted us. I was aware that the police would be scouring the neighborhoods, so we'd all agreed to change our clothes and keep a low profile. I noticed that Tommy hadn't changed his jeans. I asked him why and he told me he'd forgotten.

The bag contained £11,500. We paid the owner of the flat £1,500 and split the rest between the three of us. Then we all went our separate ways and I went to Anfield to leave my money with my friend Rava. I paid him a bonus and asked him if he'd go to Cantril Farm later in the evening and pour petrol on the Bedford van and set it on fire. He agreed, but unfortunately, the police got to the van before he did.

That night, I went to The Broadway Pub in Norris Green to see Tommy. As I walked in, I saw Tommy at the bar, but out of the corner of my eye, I saw two detectives sitting at a table. They stood out like a sore thumb in their shirts and ties. Tommy approached me smiling and I told him to get away from me.

The next morning, Tommy's house was raided by the Serious Crime Squad. Five armed officers ransacked his home and pulled both him and his girlfriend out of bed. They were about to leave but one of them looked inside a box of cornflakes and found £3,000 at the bottom of it. Tommy was arrested and charged with robbery with force. He was remanded at Risley Remand Centre and later sentenced to seven years in prison.

CHAPTER 15
GLASS, BLOOD AND MILK

With Tommy now out of the picture, John and I concentrated on the main prize. The van would leave the Girobank and arrive at the Post Office in Sefton at exactly seven minutes past nine. We'd strike at the end of April, when the van contained double its usual haul of cash due to the Easter holidays. John and I would be waiting, and with some planning and a little bit of luck, we'd hopefully end the day £75,000-£100,000 richer.

For the next two months, we planned and trained. Daily, we'd go running, lift weights and box. I brought in three more guys: John Lee, a hard, stocky man, who was known for his penchant for violent crime, and Paul Smith, a renowned car thief and racer. He was blond and would've been tall but for his hunched back. He was an expert in evading the police. Our third member, Jack Grass, was a local taxi driver and car thief. He would be driving the second car.

The plan was as follows: the two Johns would attack the van as soon as the driver opened the back doors. They would make the driver and the escort lie face down in the back of the van. They would then throw me the bags of money and I would throw them into our car. The two Johns would then join me in the car and Paul would drive us to a remote location, where Frank would be waiting with a stolen car.

When the day came, we arrived just before the van. We were all wearing ski masks and gloves. As the van pulled up, Paul parked the car right behind it. We didn't realize how fast the driver would be in getting out of the van, and by the time the two Johns had exited the car, the driver and escort were out of the van and approaching the front door of the Post Office. John Lee ran at the driver, who was carrying the bag, and punched him hard in the face. The driver was knocked right through the window of the Post Office.

John James ran over, and along with John Lee, began to pull at the bag, but the driver wouldn't let go. I then ran to the scene and pushed John Lee out of the way. I grabbed the bag but the driver still wouldn't let go, so I dragged him into the street and pulled my claw hammer out of my jacket. I looked down at the driver. He was cut up due to the fall through the window and he was covered in blood. I pleaded with him to let go, and when he saw the hammer, he did as I asked.

Paul pulled the car up next to me, but the customers, who had been in the queue for the Post Office, had run to a nearby milk float and began throwing milk bottles at us. Bottles of milk were smashing on the road and onto the car with a few of the bottles hitting us. We were covered in glass, blood and milk. We managed to get into the car and Paul sped away.

We reached our rendezvous a short time later and saw Frank waiting for us in his taxi. There was a construction site across the street and a guy was mixing cement. We all scrambled out of the car. There was blood and milk everywhere. I noticed that the guy mixing cement was writing down the number of Frank's taxi. This was bad. I began to scream at Frank. We all crammed into Frank's taxi, and as he drove away, we all peeled off our ski masks.

When Frank had driven approximately two miles, I told him to stop the car. John and I exited and took the bag with us. I told Frank that, when the police came to interview him, he should tell them he had picked us up at the side of the road as a fare.

John and I ran. We jumped over fences and ran down alleyways until we got to our safe house. It was a beautiful, three-bedroom terraced house, owned by my old friend, Thomas Munn, whom I had met as a young man in Borstal.

Thomas led John and me to a bedroom, where we changed our clothes. We opened the bag. It contained £33,000. We waited in that bedroom all day long, and in the evening, Thomas went out to the local shop and came back with a copy of the local newspaper, The Liverpool Echo. We were front-page news. The article did state, however, that we'd made off with just £13,000!

The following day, we paid Thomas £2,000, rented a car from an agency at Liverpool Airport, and decided to travel to Canning Town in the East End of London to hide out with a couple of bank robbers I knew. Just before we left the city, I made my way to a phone box and called Jimmy, a local lawyer I knew. I asked him to go to the police station on St. Anne's Street and find out if anyone had been arrested for the robbery. I told him I'd call back in an hour for him to tell me the news. When I called Jimmy back, he told me that Jack Grass had been arrested and charged with the robbery.

We arrived in London at 11 pm, just in time to have a pint in The Royal Oak pub. My friend Bobby was waiting for us. He was a bank robber I'd met while serving time in Wormwood Scrubs. Bobby let us stay at his house for seven days. We went shopping the first day, then, for the next six days, we trained in the boxing gym above the pub in the daytime and we partied at night.

We couldn't stay in London forever, so on the seventh day, we headed back to Liverpool. On my first day back, I decided to go to The Farmer's Arms pub in Club Moore. A man I knew from the neighborhood approached me and asked if I knew where Frank's money was. This particular guy had been to a party at my flat a few years earlier. I reasoned that, if he was asking me where the money was, then he, or someone close to him, had already informed the police of where I lived. The next morning, my home was raided by six members of the Serious Crimes Squad. They took me to the local police station and charged me with robbery with force.

CHAPTER 16
THE TRIAL

From the police station, I was taken to the underground bridewell, that cold, dismal purgatory, knowing full-well that I wouldn't be given bail. It was no surprise when I was informed that the hell known as Risley Remand Centre was my next destination.

I knew the place like the back of my hand and seemingly everyone in the place knew about me. Being a bank robber was one of the more respected professions in the British underworld, so right from the time I arrived, I was treated with respect.

On one of my first days in Risley, I was approached by Tommy Commerford. Tommy was a well-known and respected bank robber, who had been sentenced to ten years in prison during the 1960s for robbing Barclay's Bank on Water Street in the City Centre of Liverpool. He'd covertly entered the bank in the dead of night and drilled out all the safety deposit boxes. The job was the thing of legends. Tommy told me I was the number one bank robber of this generation.

My cellmate was Jacko Fitzpatrick. Jacko had been arrested for hijacking an armored van at the Withens Post Office in Cantril Farm. It was a robbery that netted Jacko and his team £65,000. I found it ironic that we were in on the same charges. Jacko asked me if I'd applied for "Judge in Chambers." I had no idea what that meant. He told me that, if I applied in the main office of the prison, my case might be heard before a panel of judges, who would consider the evidence against me and then make a recommendation on how to proceed. I did just as he told me to, and within two weeks, my case was brought before a panel of three judges in London. One of them, Judge Temple, stated that there wasn't enough evidence against me and suggested that

I be released.

The only evidence against me was the result of an identity parade. A 68-year-old woman had picked me out of a line-up. There was no other evidence. I was released at midday on a Saturday in October of 1979. I knew the police had influenced her decision in some way and I was hopeful I could use that to my advantage in court.

The trial was set for the first week in December. I secured a prominent barrister, David Brown QC, and a junior barrister, David Turner, and met them in my solicitor's office. They informed me that Judge Temple would be arriving from London to hear the case.

On the first day of the trial, I woke up at 6 am. My wife, Annette, made me some toast for breakfast. I didn't want to eat much. My stomach was churning.

I wore a navy-blue suit, a light-blue shirt, and a black tie. I made sure my hair was cut short, with a razor parting on the side. This was the style the cops wore. It was a big part of my plan.

Annette and I arrived at the courthouse at 8.30 am. The public gallery was full. My solicitor informed me that my trial had made the news and was one of the most high-profile trials in Liverpool. The entire case relied on the testimony of Elsie Seanor, the woman who'd picked me out of the line-up, just weeks earlier. To my absolute surprise, she was sitting by herself in the waiting room, just near the entry to the court room. Her gray hair, rotund frame, and bottle-top eyeglasses were unmistakable. The police were chatting in a huddle at the front of the court room and were deep in conversation, oblivious to anything else.

I slowly made my way outside to the waiting room and stood directly in front of her.

"Good morning, Mrs. Seanor, I'm Detective Smith. Do you remember me from the police station?" I asked in a professional manner.

She nodded in acknowledgement and I told her that everything was going to be alright. Inside the courtroom, we were called to order and silence flooded the building. In the dock, I was asked to state my name, address, and age.

The prosecutor told the jury that he was going to prove I had committed the robbery because a witness to the robbery had identified me after my arrest. He then called for the bailiff to escort Mrs. Seanor into the courtroom from the waiting room. Elsie shuffled in, flanked by the bailiff. She grunted as she stepped up into the witness box. The Prosecutor took a deep breath.

"Mrs. Seanor," he said, "can you please identify the man in the dock?"

"Oh yes," she replied. "That's Detective Smith from the police station."

The crowd in the gallery gasped in unison. The Prosecutor's mouth was wide open in confusion and horror. Judge Temple removed his glasses and rubbed his eyes with his thumb and forefinger. He instructed the jury that he couldn't let the trial go on, due to lack of evidence.

The crowd began to cheer and the cops shook their heads in disgust. The judge directed the clerk of the court to pronounce me Not Guilty and I was free to go. I walked through the court and out onto the street, arm in arm with Annette, as people came from all sides to shake my hand and wish me well.

As for Jack Grass, the driver, he did a deal with the police and became an informer. He was given three years of probation in exchange for his testimony against me and probably a few others.

CHAPTER 17
THE LIVERPOOL MAFIA

I was a free man, but news of my lucky courtroom break had reverberated through the Liverpool underground and some of the most notorious bank robbers wanted me on their teams. One of these bank robbers was Tommy Commerford, who was out on bail for his part in a massive marijuana importation scheme, known as The Kenya Connection.

Another was Tommy Hines, a bank robber who'd shot a man with a shotgun in Liverpool and blown the guy's leg off. The bouncers in the nightclub, being gangsters themselves, grabbed Tommy and sliced him up. They then rolled him in blankets and dropped him outside the door of the Liverpool Infirmary. I'd originally met him in Walton Prison, where he was serving seven years for the shooting and three years for armed robbery. We went to physiotherapy together.

I decided my best bet was to start a gang with a guy I'd known from Scotland Road as a kid, Joey Wright. Joey had a reputation for being tough. He was short and stocky with piercing blue eyes. Joey told me he had two other lads who'd be interested in being in a gang and asked me to meet them in The Throstles Nest pub on Scotland Road.

I prefer not to name the other two men, but by the end of our meeting, we had a plan firmly set. For months, we hijacked armored security vans all over Lancashire and Cheshire. All the jobs went without a hitch, until one fateful Monday evening.

Manweb was a shop located on the third floor of a shopping center in Rochdale. Throughout the weekend, people would pay their electricity bills in the shop, and on Monday evenings, a security guard wearing a helmet would arrive and trudge up the stairs with an armored box to collect the money.

Our plan was simple. We would have one member of the gang waiting in the car right below the stairs in the car park, one member on the stairs, and Joey and me right outside the door of the shop, waiting for the security guard so we could snatch the box and run. We peered through the door and saw the security guard walking towards the door. We put on our masks and I gently caressed the handle of the claw hammer I had in the inside pocket of my overcoat with my gloved hand. All was going to plan until the security guard got closer to the door. He was massive; about 6ft. 4in. tall and built like a tank. I saw Joey hesitate and move away from the door slightly. I'd never seen him like that before.

As the guard walked through the door, I jumped behind him, grabbed him by the neck and pulled him down. He then hit me square in the face with the box. Joey wrestled the box away from him, and in a panic, threw it over the wall, into the car park three floors below.

The guard got to his feet and started raining punches down on my head. I pushed him away with my legs and managed to pull his helmet off. I began ponding him on the head with the helmet. Joey then began kicking the guard until he fell to the floor. I grabbed Joey and pulled him away. We scrambled down the stairs and dove into the waiting car. Luckily, the driver had retrieved the box. We sped off towards Liverpool and could hear the distant sound of sirens as we fled.

We made our way to Huyton. We'd arranged to count and sort the cash in a safe house on Pennard Avenue, located on the notorious Blue Bell Council Estate. The robbery netted us just under £20,000. We divided the money equally and parted ways.

Our next job was a heist at the Trustee Savings Bank on Scotland Road. We'd been following an armored van for weeks and knew it would arrive at the bank at exactly 1.30 pm on Monday to deliver the money for the pensioners, who'd be waiting patiently in line when the van arrived. The three of us got there at 1.25 pm on foot and Joey parked across the street in an unassuming Bedford van.

This job had been talked through and rehearsed meticulously. I waited in line. The van arrived on time. The driver got out, walked to the rear of the van and banged on the door. The door opened and a guard inside the van handed the driver a box. At that point, one of our gang ran at the guard and charged him, knocking him onto the ground. I grabbed the box, ran across the street and climbed into the waiting Bedford van. The other two guys were nowhere in sight. They must've just run away.

Joey drove down Stanley Road and up Everton Valley. A police car passed us with sirens blazing. Joey looked into the rear-view mirror and told me the car was turning around. The police were chasing us. We gained some distance, parked the van a few streets from the safe house and exited the vehicle. I had the box. I ran through gardens and back alleys until I got to the safe house and noticed the door was already open. I ran inside and closed the door, but Joey had disappeared.

The safe house had been converted into flats. I lay on the floor in silence next to the door. I could hear the police outside. Someone had seen me enter and had alerted to police to my presence. They knew where I was and they were advancing.

There were three flats in the building and my friend lived on the third floor. I tip-toed up the stairs and quietly locked myself into the flat. The police smashed down the front door of the building and I could hear them bounding up the stairs. I heard doors being kicked in and the sound of numerous men yelling. The door to the third-floor flat burst open and cops poured in. They pinned me to the floor and cuffed my hands behind my back.

They took me to Walton Police Station, where Detective Inspectors Bailey, Walker and Smith were waiting for me in an interrogation room. They seemed well pleased. They asked me a series of questions but I zoned out and remained silent. They charged me with Robbery with Force and placed me in a cell. I could hear Joey calling my name.

At 3 am, Joey and I were escorted naked, with nothing but a blanket around us, to the bridewell in the city center. We sat there all night, and at 9 am, we were given clothes and paraded before the magistrate, who sent us back to Risley.

Joey had a plan. He told me Detective Smith was a friend of his, and for £1,500, the police would not show up to court to oppose bail at our next hearing. That would ensure we'd set free.

Two weeks later, Joey and I arrived at the Magistrate's Court and the police didn't show. The magistrate, Judge Wooten, didn't want to let us out on bail. He was grumpy at the best of times, but this time, he was fuming. He didn't want to release us, but without the police, he had no other choice. He kept us there waiting until just after 2 pm and then released us, unconditionally, on bail.

Annette was waiting for me in the car outside the courthouse and two of Joey's gangster friends were waiting for him. I asked him where he was going. He told me he was going home. I asked Annette to wait for me and I walked with Joey for a few blocks. His demeanor had changed and I was concerned about him. Eventually, I saw Detective Smith's car on the side of the road and I stopped walking with Joey and his mates. He went towards the car and began to chat with Smith, as if they were old friends.

I didn't know what to make of the encounter. By the time I got back to Annette, waiting for me in the car, I had an uneasy feeling about Joey, whom we came to refer to as the Reservoir Dog.

I was out on bail but the gang still had a job to do. We'd planned a heist at Barclays Bank on Williamson's Square in Liverpool City Centre. This was the bank Tommy Commerford had hit in the 1960s, and since then, security had been tightened. Police officers with German Shepherds were used to patrol the grounds and the alarm system was as sophisticated as it could be.

We'd worked on our plan for this job for months. At 9 am on the dot, an armored van would show up at the bank to pick up a bunch of cash, approximately £84,000. This was to be taken to a nearby construction site, where the money would be distributed to the various workers as their wages.

Joey decided he didn't want to do this job, so the three of us went ahead with our schedule without him. We pulled up in a Ford Cortina, about 50 feet behind the armored van. I got out of the car and another member of the gang accompanied me.

The driver of the van got out and entered the bank. Within a few minutes, he walked out of the bank towards the van. I ran at him and snatched the box. As I turned to run towards our car, a police vehicle pulled into the driveway of the bank.

The chase was on. I ran through the city center, on to Old Hall Street, and straight into a car park. I threw the box under a parked car and hid behind it until I thought the coast was clear. I took off my mask and overcoat and dumped them, along with my claw hammer, in a nearby garbage can. I took a bus to my brother's house and had a cup of tea with him. Later in the evening, I called a friend, and together, we drove to the car park, but the box was gone. I then got him to drop me off at the getaway driver's house on Scotland Road.

When he found out the box was gone, he lost his mind. We both knew the police had been tipped off and the only person who could've snitched was Joey Wright. We vowed revenge, and much later, we accomplished it.

CHAPTER 18
THE LUCKIEST DAY OF MY LIFE

In 1980, I was 23 years old. Things were beginning to come together beautifully. I'd been married to Annette for two years. We absolutely adored one another. I was out on bail, but I'd beaten the system before. I was adamant I could beat it again.

The world had just been introduced to the future wife of Charles, The Prince of Wales, Lady Diana Spencer. She was an exquisite blonde, with a regal gait. Although she was softly-spoken and appeared shy and kind, her inner, feminine strength shone out from her for all the world to see. Annette resembled her on all fronts.

We lived in Moss Craig flats on the Cantril Farm estate. It was government housing, but that was ok. It was a major step up from the barely furnished flat my parents, my siblings and I were crammed into at the start of my life. Our home was also far more luxurious than the cemetery I often slept in when things got tough as a child!

The first-floor flat we had was like a penthouse. It was spacious, with two bedrooms and furnished with the best: black leather Chesterfield couches and mahogany cabinets rested on dark brown shag pile carpets in the living room, while the master bedroom contained a king-sized bed and was decorated in soft pastel colors.

Life was simple and we were happy. Mornings were my favorite time of the day. Annette and I would wake up together. We'd sit and chat over a breakfast of tea and toast and then I'd drive her to her job as a receptionist at Lloyd's Bank in the city center in my orange Volkswagen Beetle.

On Monday, December 8th, 1980, Liverpool's most cherished son, John Lennon, was gunned down in New York City, leaving the whole of Britain mourning. Two days after his untimely death, our own idyllic lives took a turn that would throw us into utter turmoil.

On the Wednesday after Lennon's death, Annette and I were sleeping peacefully side by side, as we always did. I was awoken by the sound of the front door to our flat crashing violently off its hinges. My eyes opened wide and my heart began pounding immediately. I froze in place as the bedroom door slammed open and four gruff-looking men stormed into our bedroom. They were wearing business suits. Due to the cold, winter morning, they'd covered their suits with heavy, green Parker jackets.

The guy in the lead was pointing a Browning nine-millimeter, semi-automatic pistol at my head. They were a team from the Criminal Investigations Division of the Liverpool Police Constabulary's Serious Crimes Squad. There were six of them in total. The other two were clearing the flat, while the four-man team in front of me dragged me out of bed. Annette was crying. She too had been violently woken up and was beside herself with embarrassment and fear.

I tried to keep her calm, all the while forcing myself to maintain my composure. 'Keep calm' was my inner mantra. You've been through this before. Don't say a word. Tell them nothing.

"It's ok, love," I said softly. "I'll be home soon. Try not to worry."

They handcuffed my wrists at the front, threw a gray blanket over me and ushered me out of the flat, down the stairs, and into one of the two unmarked Ford Escorts they'd arrived in. We were at Liverpool Police Headquarters on St. Anne Street less than 15 minutes later. We entered through a side door into an interrogation room.

They sat me on a folding chair in the windowless room and four of them sat across the table from me. They all brandished pens and had their notebooks ready to jot down any information that might be used against me. The room was lit by a single, uncovered, sixty-watt bulb, which hung over the center of the table.

There I was, in nothing but my boxer shorts and covered with a blanket, my hands in cuffs resting on my lap. My heart was pounding out of my chest, but I was damned if I would give them the satisfaction of watching my inner turmoil being displayed on the surface.

My tormentors all looked the same to me. They were nothing more than government clones, paid to keep the little people in their place. They sat there in their gray suits, calmly preparing themselves to send me on another horrific tour of hell, but this time, they wanted to send me there for decades.

"You know why we're here, don't you, Terry?" one of them said.

Stay quiet, I told myself repeatedly. My interrogator and I locked eyes. After a few seconds, his scowl turned to a grin and he shook his head.

"Let's just cut to the chase," said another. "We know you robbed the Securicor Van on Williamson Square last week. There were witnesses, Terry. You're going down for armed robbery."

I broke my vow of silence. "I won't talk without my solicitor present. I need to call Robert Brody."

"He's on his way, Terry, but we already have you bang to rights. If you just come clean and admit it, we'll do you a deal. You'll be out in less than ten years. You'll still be a young man when you're out, Terry. Come on, do yourself a favor."

"I'll wait for Mr. Brody," I replied.

"Relax, he's on the way," said a voice in front of me.

Another one took a file off his knee and casually flicked through it. He dropped it on the table and leaned back in his chair.

"You're already out on bail for the TSB Bank job. You know you'll be going down for that with your friend, Joseph Wright. The two jobs are almost identical, Terry. We have you, you have to know that. If you give us a confession right now, we'll guarantee you'll do minimum time. If you fuck around with us, we'll nail you. I swear to God, Terry, we'll make sure you're banged up until you're an old man."

Keep quiet. Tell them nothing, I told myself.

He softened his tone and opened the file again, shaking his

head in an effort to appear more sympathetic. He looked up and gazed into my eyes.

"I can see you've had it rough, Terry, mate." He glanced down again, flicked through the file again and then resumed. "You were sentenced to three, three-year terms in the approved schools, then detention for six months, then Borstal for two years. Christ, Terry, you had it rough as a kid. Let's just end it here. You're gonna have to do some time but let that be the end of it. It's got to be hard on your head, living this kind of life. We can help you put it behind you."

He sat there staring at me for a few seconds. When I looked away and shook my head, his hard edge returned.

"Please yourself then, Terry. If you don't want to cooperate, we'll make sure you pay the full price."

I was in a panic. My head felt like it was about to explode, but I had to remain calm. My only chance was to keep my mouth shut. Every hour, two of them left the room and two more took their places. This pattern repeated itself all day. Halfway through the day, they fed me a ham sandwich and a cup of tea and then went straight back to business.

"Where's my solicitor? I won't talk without him," I said calmly, trying desperately to instill a modicum of serenity into my mind.

"He's on the way."

That was their constant reply. I knew full well I was on my own. I just had to stay the course and tell them absolutely nothing. It felt like I'd been in there for days. I felt mentally frail as the memories of my past incarcerations swirled in my mind's eye. I wanted this to end. I really didn't think I could hold out much longer.

Then it happened. The door swung open and one of Her Majesty's clones walked in. He looked at his watch and flicked his head in the direction of the outside world.

"Come on. Let's get him charged."

They took me by the arms, walked me out of the interrogation room and presented me to the uniformed Desk Sergeant. Two of the detectives held me by the arms and two approached the desk.

"We're gonna charge him with armed robbery at Barclay's Bank in the city center," said one of them.

"We can't keep him," said the Desk Sergeant stoically.

"What?"

"There's a prison officers' strike. They're not accepting new prisoners and the jail here's full, so we can't keep him."

"What'll we do with him, then?"

The Desk Sergeant rubbed his chin. "You'll have to release him and order him to come back here at 6 pm tomorrow evening."

The detective stood there with a look of shock on his face. I couldn't believe what I was hearing.

"No, no, we can't let him go. He's being done for armed robbery, for crying out loud. He's wanted for three robberies: Ford's car plant, Withens Post Office, and The Giro in Bootle. The man's a flight risk, for fuck's sake."

"I won't tell you again, detective. He can't stay here."

One of them took me into a room and took off the handcuffs that were digging into my wrists. A pile of clothes one of them had been given by Annette was waiting for me on a table.

"Get dressed," he said sternly and he left the room.

I couldn't believe my luck. They were actually letting me go! My mind switched from the morose recollections of an abused and imprisoned youth to forging a plan that would ensure my freedom from now until the end of my days. I knew one thing for sure; there was absolutely no chance in hell I was coming back to this place without being forced again at gun-point.

I casually walked out of the room and towards the Desk Sergeant's desk.

"Ok, Mr. Moogan, you're to report back here at 1800 hours tomorrow. Do you understand?"

I nodded at him and slowly strolled out of the building into the cold wind and rain of the Northern English evening. I jumped into the backseat of a taxi and ordered him to take me home.

Annette was waiting for me when I got back. As I came through the front door, she ran at me and embraced me. I could feel her entire body shivering with fear. I gently took her by the shoulders and ushered her into the living room. I sat her on the couch and knelt in front of her, my hands resting on her knees.

"I need you to listen, my love," I said as calmly as possible.

She nodded in response.

"I need you to pack a suitcase for me and make sure there's cash in it. I'm leaving now, but when I come back, I'm going to take you to your mother's for the night, and tomorrow morning, I need you to drive to Heathrow Airport. You have to be there no later than 8 am. Do you understand me, my love?"

Again, she nodded in response. I softly lifted her to her feet and hugged her one last time before leaving. I grabbed a small stash of cash from a drawer, ran down the stairs and out to the waiting taxi.

"Scotland Road," I said.

The driver must've sensed the urgency in my tone because he sped away through the rain. The rear window of the taxi was being pelted hard with raindrops, but I was constantly looking back, trying desperately to see if I was being followed.

I pointed out a house and told the driver to stop. I threw him a ten-pound note and ran from the taxi. I jumped over the fence, ran past the house and over the back wall. I landed on my feet and crouched down. I was in a back alley now. I turned my head and looked to the far end of the alley. I was soaking wet, but the rain was my friend as it gave me a modicum of protection against being followed.

I opened the gate in front of me and closed it silently as I entered the familiar back yard of my friend, Tommy Gilday. I could see the television flickering through the window. I softly knocked on the door, and within seconds, he welcomed me into his home.

Tommy Gilday and I were good friends. He was a notorious up-and-coming member of the Liverpool underworld. His short, wide muscular frame, scarred face, and cropped blond hair gave him the appearance of being hard. He was exactly what he appeared to be.

He led me from the kitchen into the living room, where another friend of mine, Egga London, was already sitting on the couch. Jimmy was a mild-mannered rogue, who had served time with me in the horrific institutions for young offenders, known as Borstal. He was tall and slender, with silky dark hair and a constant smile on his face. I was in luck. If I had the choice of any two guys to help me out of my current situation, it'd be these two.

"Sit down, Terry," said Tommy as he gave me a tea towel to dry my face. He could see the stress in my expression and tried to calm me as only a true friend would. "What's going on, mate?"

"I need you to get me to Heathrow in the morning. If I don't leave the country, I'll be going down for a long stretch."

"Ok, we could go right now, if you want?" he said. He looked at Jimmy, who smiled back and nodded his approval.

"No, I need to pick some things up from the flat," I said. "Can you meet me at 4 am in the alley behind the field across from the flats?"

"We'll be there, mate," said Tommy. "Do you want me to give you a lift home?"

"Yes," I said, "but pull the car around to the back of the house and pick me up there. You can drop me off a few streets away from the flat and I'll walk the rest of the way. The coppers are probably watching the flat."

When I got home, I filled a sports bag with a few of my most precious possessions: my gold Longines watch, some gold chains and other random pieces of jewelry. I stuffed them all into a zippered pocket on the side of the bag.

I spent the rest of the evening sitting on the couch and looking at the possessions Annette and I had amassed during our time together; the furniture, carpets and entertainment system were all top-notch. This was our home. It was our place of refuge and now I was leaving it for good, and her, for the next few months. I stared at the photos on the walls; our faces were happy, we were holding each other tightly. I was gripped by melancholy as I realized that our lives would never be the same again.

At 3.15 the next morning, I dressed in jeans, a yellow Ben Sherman shirt, and light-blue Puma trainers. I grabbed my sports bag, opened the kitchen window, and with my bag pulled tightly over my shoulder, eased myself out of the window. I grabbed the window ledge with both hands and lowered my body as far as I could, then dropped the remaining ten feet onto the concrete pavement. I landed on my feet, ran across the field and through the alley to where my friends, Tommy and Jimmy, were already waiting for me in Tommy's Ford Cortina.

It took three-and-a-half hours to get to Heathrow. We entertained ourselves along the way with jokes and reminisced through stories of the not-so-good old days. The further I got from Liverpool, the more relaxed I became. I was almost away. I was almost free.

When we arrived at the Pan Am terminal, I shook hands with the lads, grabbed my bag and quickly left them at the curb. After all, if I was to be caught now, I didn't want the lads to be pulled into the whole sordid mess. The faster they left the airport, the safer they'd be.

As I entered the terminal, I saw Annette waiting for me. As soon as our eyes met, she ran to me. We embraced and I lifted her off her feet. We walked arm in arm to the Pan Am desk. I opted to pay for a round-trip ticket to avoid scrutiny. I already had a ten-year visa attached to my passport, as a result of a trip to Miami the previous year. Annette gave me a small pouch containing £45,000 we'd stashed at her mother's for a rainy day. I covertly placed it in my bag, but not before taking out just enough money to pay for the ticket. It was a flawless transaction.

Annette and I then sat at a table and drank coffee. I could see the situation had taken a toll on her and it broke my heart. I held her hand across the table and tried to reassure her that everything was going to be alright.

"I'm going to set things up for us, love, and in a few months, you can come and join me. We'll start a new life in California," I said, trying desperately not to tear up.

She nodded and agreed, but I knew she was hurt. She had a good life in Liverpool, and although I knew she loved me dearly, she'd have to leave her other loves; her parents, her job and the wonderful home we'd built together.

"I have to leave, Terry," she said. "I've got things to do."

I nodded. We stood and embraced. We stared at each other and tried to smile, but the smiles turned to tears. She pulled herself away and walked off towards the exit. I turned my head away. I couldn't watch her leave. It was just too painful.

I sat there for a few more hours until my flight was called. When I entered the plane and took my seat, I knew I'd made it. I was now en route to a new life in sunny Southern California and soon I'd be joined by my beautiful wife. The future looked bright and I could leave my life of crime and despair where it belonged, in the past.

Years later, I was told the police had been to the site of the second bank robbery and taken fragments from the broken glasses of one of the delivery drivers and sprinkled them onto the clothes they took as evidence from my home. If I had stayed, this forged forensic evidence would've been used against me and I would've spent decades in Her Majesty's dank, cold, archaic and brutal prison system. Although I didn't feel it at the time, this was truly the luckiest day of my life.

CHAPTER 19
SERENDIPITY

The flight to Los Angeles was maddening. The plane was almost empty, so I sprawled across a whole row of seats, trying in vain to get just a few hours of quality sleep. My mind was racing, trying to make sense of this new predicament. I wondered if I'd ever see Annette again. Thoughts swirled around in my head: what if the authorities caught up with me? What if Annette decided to stay home?

The list of questions grew and none of them seemed to have favorable answers. During one of my many stays in Her Majesty's institutions, I'd formed a friendship with the great train robber, Gordon Goody. He'd become a mentor to me. He would often urge me to stay calm and his presence alone usually did the trick. I envisioned him in my mind's eye.

"Stay calm," I whispered to myself.

Outwardly, the flight attendants and other passengers were unaware of my anguish, but inside, I was in the middle of a nervous breakdown.

I arrived in Los Angeles in the early afternoon and just breezed past the customs and immigration desk. I changed some English pounds into dollars and headed out into the sunlight. I sat on a bench and closed my eyes as I turned my face upward towards the sun. I'd just left the cold, wet weather of Northern England and here I was, in the warm, arid sunlight of Southern California. On the surface, I suppose I looked like a tourist on vacation, but inwardly, I was a man on the run and no amount of sunshine would be able to block that from my thoughts.

I opened my eyes and jumped into the first taxi I saw.

"Take me to Santa Monica, please mate," I asked.

"Where in Santa Monica?" he responded, staring at me through the rear-view mirror.

I paused for a while and collected my thoughts. "Take me to a hotel near the beach," I said, and we were off.

He dropped me at The Hotel Carmel on the corner of Broadway and Second streets. The beige building was classy and low-key, built in the Spanish revival style. It was comfortable, chic, and most importantly, affordable. I checked in for a week and was charged twenty-two dollars a night for the privilege. The receptionist was cute, blonde, and friendly.

"Is there anywhere close to get a drink?" I asked.

"There's an English pub next door," she said with a smile.

I ran up the stairs to my room and left my bag on the bed, but not before stashing the money I'd brought into the safe.

The Cheshire Fox was the real deal when it came to pubs. Dark wood tables and chairs filled the floor space and the central bar was made of oak and finished with brass rails. There were a few people eating dinner, but no one was sitting at the bar, where I took a seat. The young, blonde barmaid instantly bombarded me with conversation. She was hilarious and loud, the prefect distraction for my predicament. She poured me a pint of lager.

"Our chef's from England," she said, and without another beat, she screeched into the kitchen, "Jimmy, there's a guy in here from England!"

The door to the kitchen swung open and a short, chubby man of about forty, with thinning black hair and a dirty black t-shirt, walked in behind the bar. He wiped his hands on his shirt and held out the right one.

"Jimmy," he said.

I introduced myself and we spent a bit of time chatting. He told me he was from Manchester, and when he asked me if I was on vacation, I told him about my time as a butler on the luxury cruise liner, The Queen Elizabeth II. I reminisced about my days in service to such stars as Elizabeth Taylor and her husband, Richard Burton. I informed him how she'd urged me to become an actor, or at the very least, a butler in Beverly Hills. I told him that, during one of our many intimate conversations, she'd recommended that I visit Santa Monica, so here I was, sitting in The Cheshire Fox pub, drinking a pint and all at the request of Elizabeth Taylor.

Jimmy laughed and shook his head at my story. He cooked me fish and chips for dinner, and after I finished them off, I knocked back the last dregs of my pint and told him I was going to bed. I approached the front door to leave the pub, but Jimmy shouted out to me.

"Hey, Terry," he said, "there's another English pub right up the street on Santa Monica Boulevard, between 5th and 6th streets. It's called The King George V. Another guy from Liverpool works there."

"Ok," I said. "I'll pop in there tomorrow."

I didn't sleep well on my first night in Santa Monica, but I got enough sleep to be able to function. The chat I'd had with Jimmy settled me a little bit. I ate breakfast and walked the two blocks to the pier and then along Ocean Avenue. I instantly fell in love with the place. The Pacific Ocean was at my flank as I gazed at the legion of palm trees planted symmetrically on both sides of the street. I walked for a few miles and then decided to take Jimmy's advice and get some lunch at The King George V.

It was easy to find. I followed the directions Jimmy had given me, walking up Santa Monica Boulevard and right there, on the corner of Fifth and Sixth streets, it stood. A portrait of the king himself hung on a sign mounted on the wall outside, flanked by the Union Flag on one side and Old Glory on the other.

The pub had a similar ambiance to The Cheshire Fox. Pewter tankards hung on hooks by their handles over the oval bar. An older man in his 60s, with white, wispy hair and a long white beard, greeted me from behind the bar as I walked in.

"What ya want, mate?" he said with an East London accent.

"Have you got any breakfast?" I replied, as I sat at the bar.

When he heard my accent, his face beamed. "You're a fuckin'

scouser," he announced, referring to the term most people from Britain use when referring to people from Liverpool. "There's a fuckin' scouser in the kitchen." He screamed into the kitchen, "Eddie, there's another scouser in the bar!"

A tall, dark-haired, good-looking man with a broken nose walked out of the kitchen and behind the bar. He looked tough and clearly kept himself in shape. He stared at me for a few seconds and then looked me straight in the eye.

"I know you," he said. "You're Alan Moogan's brother."

I was gob-smacked. I shook my head.

"I've slept on your mother's couch after a night on the piss," he said with a smile. "You're Terry Moogan."

I shook my head again, trying as hard as I could to remember him.

"I'm Eddie Creed, Derek Creed's brother."

Derek Creed was a good friend of mine. Now I knew who the guy in front of me was.

"To tell you the truth, Eddie, I'm fucking starving," I said, trying to make light of the situation.

Eddie nodded and told me he'd make me some breakfast. I sat at a table and he joined me for the meal, just like he was another customer.

He seemed to know almost everything about me. He told me that he too was a victim of the Approved School and Borstal systems of juvenile "criminal justice." We instantly connected and we chatted for hours. When he asked me what I was doing in California, I tried to be as vague as possible. I told him I couldn't go back and asked for his discretion. During our chat, a couple walked in. They were both in their 40s.

"This is Gladys and Victor. They bought the pub two months ago," said Eddie.

I shook their hands, and as they introduced themselves to me, I detected an accent.

"Where are you from?" I asked.

"We're from Norway," said Victor. "The last owners were Scottish."

"Terry's gonna be working the 4-10 pm shift," said Eddie. He shot me a wink. "Terry's been a butler on the QEII and knows this industry like the back of his hand, don't you, Terry?"

"Yes. I've got plenty of experience," I said nonchalantly.

Gladys and Victor seemed overjoyed at the prospect of employing me. They chatted for a few minutes and then disappeared off into the kitchen.

"You'll make $300 a week," he said. "Oh, and by the way, do you need somewhere to stay?"

I told him I was staying at The Hotel Carmel for a week, but I needed somewhere long-term.

"I've got a spare room in my apartment. If you want it, you can have it for $150," he said. "It's right across the street on 4th Street and Strand."

Without another thought, I answered. "I'll have it."

He looked at his watch. "I finish work at six. Meet me back here then and I'll show it to you."

I paid the bill and went for a walk. I couldn't believe my luck. It was my first full day in Santa Monica and already I'd found a job and a long-term place to live. More importantly, I'd found a trusted ally in Eddie.

I got back to the pub at just after six and Eddie was waiting. We walked across the street. His place was literally on the doorstep of the pub. The building was relatively new. The apartment was spacious and modern with black furniture. My bedroom was already furnished and the pool in the central courtyard was the perfect place to relax, far from the "madding crowd." I loved it. I spent one more night in the hotel and moved out the next day.

Over the next few months, things went well. Eddie taught me the ropes at the pub. We made steak and kidney pies, scouse pies, sausage rolls and Cornish pasties. We reorganized the kitchen, re-wrote the menu and began to take the pub to the next level. People began talking about the place and the local media got involved. Eddie and I became great friends; the best. I confided in him and told him I was on the run.

One day, six Welshmen came in and began causing a ruckus. They were working on a local building project and had been in for food and drinks before. I was working the early shift that day and Eddie had just arrived to replace me.

"Where are those fucking scousers?" one of them shouted as he entered the pub.

I could tell Eddie was a little nervous, given the fact that he'd be dealing with them alone. I tried to put him at ease.

"I'm going home to get changed, but I'll be back within the hour," I said. "If they start on you, you know where the hammers are, don't you?"

Eddie nodded. We kept a couple of claw hammers in the kitchen, just in case things got heated. I walked into the kitchen and motioned for Eddie to follow me.

"If you think they're all gonna go after you, grab a pan, scoop the fat out of the deep fat fryer, and throw it over them." I made large sweeping gestures with my hands to instruct him.

Once again, Eddie nodded.

"You'll be ok, mate," I said. "I'll be back soon, anyway."

I left the bar and went home to shower and change. After about an hour, I was walking across the street towards the bar and I noticed police squad cars outside and yellow police tape across the door. The owners were outside and talking to the police. A few of the Welshmen were outside getting bandaged up by the paramedics that had arrived in their ambulances.

I approached Victor. "What happened?" I asked.

Before he could answer, one of the Welshmen shouted over from the ambulances, "We're gonna kill that bastard!"

They wouldn't tell the police who'd attacked them with the boiling grease. A few of them were injured but not badly enough to suffer the cost of an ambulance ride or treatment at a local hospital.

I made arrangements for Eddie to stay away for a week. The next morning, the Welsh fellas came back. They were pissed and looking for Eddie's head. I made peace with them. I told them that Eddie didn't want any trouble and the only reason he did what he did was because there were six of them and only one of him. I apologized on his behalf and told the group they'd always be welcomed back. They accepted my offer.

Eddie came back to work and again things were going well. The bar was a success and Eddie and I were back on track. I'd been working at the bar for months now and I was a trusted employee. Gladys and Victor seemed to love me. I felt secure in my employment. The bar had a rental unit above it. It was nothing special, just two small rooms and a shared bathroom. Two scousers, who were an obvious couple, were renting it. One day, I arrived at work and witnessed Victor in a shouting match with them. I'd never seen him like that before. The argument seemed to be about money but I tried to ignore them as I set up the bar. Then Victor said something that put me on edge.

"I'm going to call the police and immigration," he said. I approached him and gently interjected.

"Don't say that, Victor, there's no need to go there."

He flipped out on me and berated me as he'd berated them.

"Fuck you," he said. "You're fired."

That was it. I saw red. I head-butted him and punched him repeatedly until he was a bloody mess on the floor. I ran from the pub and knew I couldn't go back to the apartment. I went to the place I'd stayed on my first night in Santa Monica, The Hotel Carmel.

Eddie came and told me that Victor had been hospitalized and wanted to press charges against me. I was absolutely crushed. For months, I had been preparing a life for my wife and me and now I'd fucked it all up with one momentary act of violence. I listened to Eddie and thought about my response as he waited.

"Tell Victor to call the cops and tell them that it was all his fault and that he wants to drop the charges," I said. "Tell him, if he doesn't do that, I'll burn his fucking pub down and he'll have nothing."

I could see Eddie was disturbed by this, but he agreed to relay the message. Within the week, Eddie told me Victor had thought the whole thing through and was prepared to drop the charges. I moved back in with Eddie and then eventually met Victor in the bar. He was still injured. His face was slightly swollen and the scar on his nose from the impact of my head was prominent. He hugged me and told me that he forgave me, but he wasn't prepared to give me my job back. It was now time to regroup and start my American experience again.

CHAPTER 20
TRAUMA FOLLOWS CLOSELY

In the weeks after my departure from The George, I experienced emotional turmoil. Every night, I had lucid dreams of the police violently arresting me at gun-point, while I was in bed. The violence I'd committed against Victor depressed and disturbed me. I'd fled to California to begin a new life, but the life I'd lived in Liverpool was following me. I promised myself that my days of violence were over, but the turmoil continued. The anxiety of being a man on the run was driving me crazy and taking a huge toll on my mental health.

I'd walk for hours every day, just to try to organize my thoughts. I'd walk down Main Street and eventually cut down to Ocean and walk along the beach. I'd then take the boardwalk from Santa Monica to Venice. One day, as I strolled down Main Street, I looked up and saw a sign that read: Muhammad Ali's Boxing Gym. I felt compelled to walk inside. As I entered, I noticed an older African-American man sitting on the side of the ring, reading a magazine. He looked up when he heard me walk through the door and greeted me with a handshake. I saw Jimmy Ellis sitting there with Muhammad Ali. I struck up a conversation with both of them, laughing together. It was amazing that I was in the presence of the greatest.

Jimmy Ellis was the former WBA heavyweight champion, who'd taken the title from Joe Frazier. He just happened to be Ali's best friend and the manager of the gym. I asked him how much it would cost to train there.

He shrugged, looked me up and down and said, "Two dollars a day."

I went home to get the small amount of boxing gear I'd brought with me from Liverpool and started training that day.

The gym was almost empty, so I trained alone; shadow boxing, bag work, skipping, and body weight exercises. Jimmy was watching. He asked me how long I'd been training and I told him I'd boxed since I was a child. Jimmy looked like he was impressed. Over the days and weeks, he held pads for me and gave me pointers here and there, helping me to hone my skills. I met and trained with some world-class boxers in that gym and even formed a friendship with the British, Commonwealth and European heavyweight champion, Joe Bugner.

A short time after I began training at the gym, I began to feel sick and weak. I literally had no energy and had a hard time making it out of bed. I coped for a few days and then decided to go to St. John's Hospital Emergency Room. They examined me at the hospital but told me that they couldn't find anything wrong. As a precaution, they sent me to a general practitioner on 15th Street. His name was Dr. Messina.

I arranged an appointment, and within a few days, I was in Dr. Messina's clinic. The moment he saw me, he knew there was something wrong. He gave me a full examination and took a blood sample, which he analyzed in a machine in his clinic during my visit. He concluded that I was anemic and that the anemia was probably the result of bleeding ulcers in my stomach. He gave me a shot of iron in the buttock and sent me off for a series of gastro-intestinal tests.

I went back to his clinic for the test results and was told I had three bleeding ulcers in my stomach. He prescribed me Sucralfate, an antacid used in the treatment of ulcers, and instructed me to come back to his clinic once a week for two months for iron injections. I began to trust Dr. Messina and decided to confide in him. I told him about my turbulent childhood, the abuse I'd suffered through in the approved school system, my time in Borstal and at other young offender institutions, and the time I'd done in prison. I then told him I was on the run.

He listened patiently, and when I finished my story, he gave me a prescription for Valium and referred me to a Forensic Psychiatrist, Dr. Ralph Obler.

Dr. Obler listened to my story, just as Dr. Messina had. He concluded that I was suffering from General Anxiety. He refilled my Valium prescription and sent me on my way. The Valium had me walking the streets in a daze and did nothing for my terrifying dreams. The nightmares continued and got worse. I was losing my mind.

I went back to Dr. Obler and told him I needed help. He prescribed me a drug called Thorazine. He told me it was usually prescribed to people who'd been hospitalized due to a mental breakdown. He said the side effects would include exhaustion to the point where I probably wouldn't be able to get out of bed. As a result of this, I declined the medication. I continued to go to Dr. Messina for my iron injections, and after two months, he sent me back to St. John's Hospital for more tests.

When the results came back, I was told my ulcers had sealed and were no longer bleeding. It was then that I told Dr. Messina about my new malady. I informed him I was getting constant, excruciating pains in my head. He referred me to a neurosurgeon at Cedars Sinai Hospital, Dr. Nelson.

Dr. Nelson examined me and performed two CT scans on my head, both of which showed no signs of damage. He concluded that I was having convulsions from the trauma I'd been subjected to for most of my life. He prescribed Dilantin, a drug used for the treatment of brain tumors. Once again, I declined the drug.

Dr. Messina and Dr. Obler monitored me for the next few years, but the medications' side effects were far worse than the afflictions they were treating. I decided, for the time being anyway, to decline the drugs and deal with my mental health the only way I knew how, through severe physical training and wearing the heavy mask of normalcy, all the while praying to God that it wouldn't slip.

CHAPTER 21
THE TUDOR HOUSE

Within a few months of me leaving The George, Eddie went off to live in New Zealand. I took over the lease of the apartment and redecorated it in anticipation of the arrival of my brother, Alan, and the love of my life, my beautiful Annette.

Now all I needed was a job. When I worked at The George, a man who we all knew as Legs would often come in for a drink and tell me that, if I ever needed a job, I could work with him at The Tudor House. At the time, I didn't need a job, but now I was ready to move on.

The Tudor House was a restaurant that sold predominantly British pies and confectionary. It was always busy, with lines of customers around the block, waiting for their take-out orders. The restaurant was unable to seat all the guests, who would wait eagerly for a table to become vacant.

I went there and asked Legs if I could get a job. I told him I'd worked for a short time as a cook and baker on the Queen Elizabeth II cruise ship and that, with just a little bit of training, I would be able to cope with the high volume of produce.

Legs told me he would teach me to make the various pies, including those I already knew: scouse pies, steak and kidney pies, sausage rolls and Cornish pasties. I would then be the pie-maker and Legs would be the main confectioner, making all the various pastries and desserts. He informed me I would be paid fifty cents for every pie sold throughout the day.

Now I had a job, and later that week, Annette and Alan arrived. I hadn't seen Annette in close to three months. There she was, walking out of the Los Angeles Airport with my brother. She and I embraced. I couldn't wait to show her the apartment.

We drove out of the airport in my big red Caddie, one of two cars I'd bought since coming to America. We took Alan to The Tudor House and I introduced him to Legs. It just so happened that Legs was leaving the country to live in New Zealand, I told my brother. Legs knew the restaurant would need to replace him, so he offered to train Alan as a confectioner, to take over his job when he was gone. Alan fitted in perfectly. He worked hard, and by the time Legs left, Alan was fully trained and well able to keep up with the demands of the job.

After we left Alan, Annette and I spent a lovely evening together, talking with great excitement about our new life. The next day, we drove up the coast to Malibu, where we had lunch and marveled at the stunning mansions on the hills in the distance. This area was where she and I would spend our nights, watching the sun go down on the horizon. It was a magic moment for us both.

Before she left England, Annette had sold all our furniture and my car and drained our bank accounts, bringing all the cash with her, as I had when I first arrived in the U.S. Her arrival was a joyous occasion for me, but for her, it was bittersweet. She loved me and wanted to be with me, but she was close to her parents, who were in their sixties at the time. The thought of leaving them in England broke her heart. She did her best to pull herself together and soon she found work as a receptionist at a large real estate company.

The owners of The Tudor House wanted to increase their profit margins, so they head-hunted a confectioner from Manchester and gave him Alan's job. Alan was then demoted to work alongside me as a pie-maker. This instantly caused discontent. The new confectioner, Steve, was, as far as we were concerned, arrogant, to say the least. We didn't get along from the get-go, but Steve made things worse with his constant demands.

He was supposed to finish making the confectionery by 6 am, to make way for Alan and me to start making the fresh pies, but he was always late, and as a result, constantly in our way. One day,

I wasn't feeling well, and when I arrived at work, I sat for a few minutes in a closet to compose myself. Steve saw me sitting there and went berserk. He screamed at me, saying that I needed to start washing his pots and pans. I politely told him that I was not his pot-washer and that his mess was his and his alone to clean up. However, Steve continued to harass me. It took every ounce of discipline I had to refrain from throwing him through the nearest window.

Steve had a habit of asking Alan and me about our immigration status. He'd throw out questions like, "What's your status?" and "What type of visa are you here on?" Alan and I knew he was using this line of questioning to intimidate us. Every time he would ask the questions, one of us would reply, "It's none of your business."

One day, I worked all morning and wanted a fish and chips lunch at The George. I asked Alan if he wanted to join me. He told me he wanted to keep working to keep up with the demands of the customers, so I left him to it and told him I'd be back within the hour.

Less than an hour later, I strolled back in through the back door and was approached by one of the waitresses. She told me to be careful because agents from the Immigration and Nationalization Service had raided the restaurant while I was at lunch and had arrested Alan. I was shocked and knew it was Steve who'd called them. I wanted to kill him, but I'd promised myself that my days of beating people up were over. I walked out of the restaurant, never to return. Alan had been taken to a holding cell in the city of Los Angeles. He was later made to stand before an immigration judge and deported back to England. If I had stayed with Alan that day, I too would've been deported.

Once again, I was out of a job. I thought about what Elizabeth Taylor had suggested when I served her on the Queen Elizabeth II.

"You should be an actor, or at the very least a butler in Beverly Hills," she said many times over, during our chats on the ship.

My confidence was through the floor. I couldn't see myself on the big screen, being idolized by the masses. Even the thought of it intimidated me, but I knew everything there was to know about service, so I chose to follow her advice and seek employment with the pre-eminent agency in Beverly Hills, The International Domestic Agency. I'd often walked past the building on Beverly Drive and thought about dropping in, so I called and made an appointment with the owner, Dora Renet.

On the following Monday morning, I left the Cadillac at home and instead drove my brand-new gray Ford Mustang to Beverly Drive. I stepped out of the car and opened the back door to take my charcoal grey suit jacket off the hanger hooked over the rear seat and brushed it down before putting it on. I reached over to the passenger seat and grabbed my Merchant Navy discharge book. I steadied myself, took a deep breath and got into character. I was a butler now and the finest butler in Beverly Hills, bar none. All I had to do was convince the owner of the agency just that and my dream would be realized. I pulled my shoulders back and walked in through the doors of The International Domestic Agency.

Dora was the founder and owner of the agency. A good-looking, classy, and professional woman of Italian descent, she had been providing the best service staff to the Hollywood elites for years. I knew she was impressed as we chatted. She scanned my face, my suit, my hands and my shoes and I could tell she was checking all the boxes as she took mental notes.

She asked me to fill out an application form and then, as she took the paperwork, I offered her the Merchant Navy discharge book I had received after my service on the QEII. She opened it up and scanned the pages thoroughly. I had been classified as a Penthouse Rooms Steward and the classification was stamped with red ink indicating "Outstanding."

She was definitely impressed. She asked about my service on The Queen Elizabeth II and I chatted about the many illustrious guests I'd serviced. She didn't ask me anything about my schooling, my life since leaving the ship, or what I'd been doing in the US during the months I'd been here.

"I have the perfect job for you," she said enthusiastically. "It's in Carmel. Do you mind flying to Monterey Airport?" she asked, while flipping through the paperwork on her desk. I shook my head.

"I don't mind at all," I said. "If you don't mind me asking, who will I be working for?" I asked.

Dora leaned across the table, peered over her glasses and smiled as she stared into my eyes. "The client is…"

CHAPTER 22
THE GOOD, THE BAD AND THE WANTED

Dora gave me the address for the interview when I was in her office the day before. I drove through the Hollywood Hills, and when I reached the large iron gates, I tapped the button on the intercom. The gates opened wide and I slowly drove up the gravel drive to the opulent, modern, glass, contemporary house. My hands fumbled around on the passenger seat, grabbing and sorting out my documents, references and, of course, my Merchant Navy discharge book.

I checked my face in the rear-view mirror. Beads of sweat had collected on my forehead. I was nervous. This interview was a big deal. Doubts once again enveloped me. I checked the mirror again and saw the remnants of the street urchin I'd once been on the infamous Scotland Road in Liverpool. I snapped myself out of the fog of self-doubt. I wiped my brow with a Kleenex from the box in the center console and exited the car.

They say that clothes don't make the man, but in this case, first impressions were crucial. I was wearing a tailored, navy-blue, single-breasted suit and a pristine white shirt, adorned with a conservative blue tie and well-polished, black brogue shoes. I knew I looked the part; now all I had to do was convince the client that I actually was the part, and there she was, waiting patiently at the open front door.

Maggie was tall and slim, with long, blonde hair and sapphire-blue eyes. She wore a pink polo-neck sweater, beige pants, and flat black shoes. She welcomed me warmly with a handshake and led me into the house, past the staircase and through a corridor, which led to an immaculate, orderly office.

She sat behind the desk and I remained standing until she

motioned with her hand for me to take a seat. We talked for a while about my time on the Queen Elizabeth II cruise ship. I told her of all the illustrious people I'd served. I showed her pictures and then my Discharge book. She seemed just as impressed as Dora had been the day before.

I told her I'd spent the first twelve months on the ship as a cook and that I'd worked my way up to the position of Penthouse Room Steward, or Butler, as we were commonly known.

Maggie told me the position I was applying for was in the coastal town of Carmel, on the 17 Mile Drive, just south of San Francisco. I had expected the position to be in Beverly Hills; after all, Annette was working as a receptionist for a real estate company and wouldn't want to leave their employ to move to Carmel. I decided then and there that I had to still push for this job, as it wasn't every day that a Liverpool scally like me got a chance to work for Maggie and Clint Eastwood.

The interview went on for two hours. Maggie told me about her children, Kyle and Alison, and I informed her that I could make a curriculum for the house and include in it duties that would involve both cooking and tending to the kids. She seemed delighted. She told me she felt relaxed around me. I knew that if Maggie had kept me chatting for this long, it meant the job was mine, but the deal wasn't sealed yet. She told me she had some phone calls to make and asked me to come back to the house in an hour. I checked my watch and happily obliged.

I had lunch in the low-key but famous Beachwood Café in Hollywood and then used the public phone to call Dora in her office. Dora told me Maggie had called her and was eager to hire me. She said Maggie especially liked my sincere interest in the well-being of her children and informed me she would offer me the job when I returned to her house.

Looking back now, I'm amazed at how little I valued my experiences and skills as a butler. I had been sure I was average, but Dora and her clients were nothing but impressed with my persona, the quintessential English Butler.

When I arrived back at the house, Maggie was eager to offer

me the job. She told me an extension had been built onto the house in Carmel and that the extension would be my living quarters.

I asked her if my wife, Annette, could come and she insisted that she would always be welcome. I also asked Maggie if she could fly me to Monterey Airport and then pick me up from there to drive me to Carmel. She agreed.

My relief and happiness at being hired to work for Client Eastwood consumed me all the way home and I couldn't wait to tell my wife all about it in detail. When I was young, I watched Client on the big screen and thought back then, What an actor! I never thought that, when I got older, I would reside in his house as his butler on the 17 Mile Drive in Carmel, California. He was a giant of a man to me, and here I was, shaking his hand in his living room, a far cry from the prison walls of England. As a man of few words, he nevertheless thanked me sincerely for taking care of his children, Alison and Kyle. I knew when he looked into my eyes that he was, indeed, a great man.

When I told Annette my news, she was just as excited as I was, but then I saw the look in her eye change from excitement to sorrow. She knew I would once again be leaving her. I came to an agreement with Annette that, at least once a month, she would come and visit me. That settled her a little but I could tell she was still upset I was leaving.

I arrived in Monterey Airport in the early afternoon on a March Monday in 1982. Maggie was outside waiting for me in Clint's long, silver Mercedes 6.9 model. I threw my bags in the trunk and off we went. We stopped along the way at her family's restaurant, The Hog's Breath Inn, and had lunch in the simple, wooden cabin-like structure.

We drove along the beautiful 17 Mile Drive. It curved exquisitely through the landscape, with green and brown pastures and trees on one side and the beaches of the Pacific Ocean on the other. We came to a set of gates that led through what looked like a dense forest of evergreens and eventually to another set of recessed gates, seemingly hidden in the foliage. The gates swung wide and the landscape opened up. A long drive lay ahead of us, flanked by finely-mown lawns, which led to the grand, old, wooden house at the end.

Maggie parked right in front of the house and I grabbed my bags from the trunk. She led me into the new extension and showed me my living quarters. The place was spacious, with new thick, dark green carpets and light, heavily-grained, wooden furniture, giving the whole place the feeling of a quaint, country cottage.

She told me to settle in, and when I was ready, to join her in the main house for a tour. I unpacked and lay on the bed for a few minutes. I'd only been away from Annette for a few hours and I already missed her. Anxiety rushed through my mind as I thought about my childhood and the trauma I'd been through. My anxiety then yielded ever so slightly as I marveled at the fact that I was in the home of the great Clint Eastwood.

Maggie answered the door to me and led me into the house. It was a genuine home. It looked lived-in, well-used, but still immaculately clean. The whole place smelled like pine needles. The living room was plain and comfortable, full of greens and browns, but what made it spectacular were the views of the beach and the great expanse of the Pacific Ocean.

We walked through a hallway and I noticed a small gym. There was a speedball mounted to the ceiling. I was impressed and I told Maggie I would teach Kyle how to use it when I got the chance.

When we got to the kitchen, Maggie asked if I could make some dinner for the children. I agreed. She took me into the rear garden and explained that wild deer often visited them and that any leftover food we had should be fed to the animals. She told me they had named one of the deer Matilda and that she was extremely precious to the family. There was also a family of raccoons who would visit daily.

I realized, when I got back to the kitchen, I had less than an hour to prepare for the children's arrival, so I got to work. I made them burgers and fries and they seemed well impressed. Kyle was approximately twelve years old and Alison was about ten. They were polite and intelligent. They complimented me on my cooking and Kyle was eager to tell me about his experiences on set with his dad, during the filming of his new movie, "Honkytonk Man." Alison was curious about the art of cooking and asked me if I would teach her. Of course, I told her that I would and advised her that her first lesson would be the fine skill of cooking scrambled eggs.

During the week, I composed a curriculum for the house, which involved a cleaning, cooking and maintenance schedule. I'd feed the kids and chat to them about their lives, school, and the various hobbies they enjoyed. Maggie brought her friends around one evening to show off her new English butler. I cooked them cranberry chicken with roast potatoes and Vichy carrots, topped off with a splash of brandy. The ladies had a fantastic time. That was the first formal dinner I'd served at the house. It went like clockwork.

On the Friday of my first week, I heard the door open and I turned to see the man himself facing me. I held out my hand.

"Pleased to meet you, Sir. I'm Terry."

He shook my hand, asked me how I was doing, and smiled. He then proceeded to sit at the kitchen counter and chat to me. We talked about his kids predominantly.

At least once a month, Annette would visit, spending Friday, Saturday and Sunday with me. We'd go for walks on the winding trails and have our meals in the local restaurants. We'd sit on the rocks at the beach in silence, holding each other close to maintain warmth amid the cold ocean breeze. I would feel like my heart had fallen out of my chest when I'd watch her disappear through the airport departure lounge at the end of her visits.

Clint would come to the house sporadically and spend most of his time there with the kids. They loved him. I could tell he was a fantastic father. He was genuinely interested in their lives and wanted to be with them. As the weeks turned to months, however, he began visiting less and less.

One Friday, Maggie asked me if I'd collect a friend of hers at Monterey Airport. I agreed and drove out there. Maggie had described me to her friend, so at the arrivals gate, he made a beeline directly for me. His name was Henry Weinberg. He was tall, with thick black hair and sallow skin. I introduced myself to him, but in return, he was short with me and seemed laconic.

I placed his bags in the little red Mercedes sports car, as he sat waiting in the passenger seat. The second I started the engine, he lit up a cigarette. I thought it a little bit rude of him to be smoking in Maggie's car. This, along with his dismissive attitude, made me instantly dislike him.

That evening, I cooked them a meal of poached salmon with broccoli and pasta, followed by an English trifle for dessert. They sat and ate intimately together. Maggie complimented me on the dinner but Weinberg said nothing.

The following day, I awoke early and cooked them scrambled eggs and bacon and served it with glasses of fresh orange juice. After breakfast, when I was alone in the kitchen, Weinberg approached me and told me to clean the windows. The windows were at least twenty feet high. I told him I was the butler and that I knew nothing of window-cleaning. He got agitated and began to interrogate me, asking me what my duties were.

Weinberg began visiting Maggie weekly. I didn't like him and felt lonely without Annette. I knew the agency would have work for me closer to home, so I decided to leave Carmel. After dropping Weinberg back at the airport one Friday, I got back to the house and told Maggie I was leaving. I told her how much I missed Annette and that I wanted to be with her. Maggie didn't want me to leave. I left on good terms. This had been a magnificent experience. The four months I'd worked for Maggie and Clint Eastwood were magical. I left Maggie the phone number for my apartment in Santa Monica and bade her farewell.

I'd been back in Santa Monica for just over a week when

Maggie called me. She asked me if I was working, and when I said I wasn't, she told me of a friend who she'd been speaking with who wanted to hire me. This conversation was to result in another celebrity adventure in Carmel, but this would involve Annette also.

CHAPTER 23
MERV GRIFFIN THE MEDIA MOGUL

I entered the lounge in the prestigious office block in the heart of Hollywood and approached the receptionist at her desk.

Without a word from me, she said, "Good morning, Mr. Moogan. Mr. Griffin will be with you in a few minutes. Please take a seat."

I was impressed by her manner and attention to detail, as both are crucial in being a successful butler and a bank robber. I sat on one of the nearby chairs and waited nervously. Merv was head-hunting me. He was a titan in the world of media. He'd begun as a radio and big band singer in the 1940s and furthered his career by creating television hits such as "Wheel of Fortune," "Jeopardy," and "The Merv Griffin Show." In other business ventures, he had acquired a number of hotels, the most prestigious being The Beverly Hilton.

Maggie had apparently told him everything about me, the curriculum I'd composed, the quality of my cooking, and the rapport I'd built with her and her family, and most importantly, my work ethic. She'd laid everything out in front of him and now he had summoned me to convince me to become his butler.

The door swung open and out walked Merv. He was a short man in his sixties with white hair and dressed impeccably in a dark blazer and beige slacks. He greeted me with a warm smile and shook my hand vigorously, while leading me into his office and then closing the door. I could tell he was excited to see me.

He got straight to business. Maggie's glowing reference had sealed the deal for him and now he just wanted to tell me the details of the position he was offering. He told me that his married butler and maid, Jack and Evelyn, were retiring and he needed to fill their positions. The job would be at his five-acre compound in Carmel.

He was a congenial man, warm and welcoming. I instantly liked him. He asked me if Annette and I would fly with him in his private jet to Monterey Airport, where Jack would collect us and take us to the property. I thought about it for a few moments and then informed him that, although I was sold on the idea, I'd have to run it by Annette before I could make a definite decision.

Annette was sold as much as I was. Just over two weeks after Merv and I first met, she and I were on the tarmac of Van Nuys Airport, ready to board Merv's luxurious Challenger CL60 private jet. He again greeted me warmly. I introduced him to Annette and he took to her instantly. He then turned to his companion, a tall, dark-skinned, good-looking man in his mid-twenties and introduced him to us as Tony. Tony was softly-spoken, and although he was friendly, he was quiet and unassuming. I knew that Merv was a gay man.

We boarded the plane and made ourselves comfortable in the beige leather seats before taking off. Merv and Tony were close. They were flirtatious with one another and were inseparable during the flight. They didn't hide the fact that they were lovers.

We arrived at Monterey Airport and were greeted by Merv's butler, Jack, who was driving a standard station wagon. Merv and Tony seemed fine with it. With all the celebrity, wealth and flash I'd seen and heard of Merv thus far, the normalcy of the station wagon seemed a little bit odd to me, but it drew me to Merv even more. It led me to believe that deep inside, he was just a down-to-earth guy.

On the drive to Carmel, Merv chatted happily about his beloved compound. The rose garden, guest cottages, and his own private house delighted him. Jack just sat and listened. Every once in a while, he'd nod or let out a laugh at an appropriate time.

We entered through the gates of the five-acre estate and I instantly felt at home. I marveled at the sheer magnitude of it. The scent of lavender gently caressed my nose. The rose garden, fields of organic orchards, and berry bushes gave the whole space a healthy and natural quality and the two acres of vineyards were reminiscent of the depictions of the south of France I'd seen.

We rolled past the quaint guest cottages and arrived at the 9,500 sq. ft. main house. Jack and I took Merv and Tony's bags inside and then Jack drove Annette and me less than 500 ft. to the house he called home, the house we would soon call home, too. It had four bedrooms and was a warm, spacious building. Jack introduced us to his wife, Evelyn. They seemed happy and content and told us they loved working for Merv. The decades of service they'd given him were an indicator of the type of employer he was.

After we unpacked and settled in to one of the guest rooms, Jack and Evelyn walked us to the main house. Merv himself took Annette and me for a tour. The walls were covered with black and white photos of Merv with all the stars he'd interviewed over the years. There were thousands of them, covering the Hollywood elite for over three decades.

At last, he led us to the dining room, where Jack, Evelyn and Tony were waiting for us. This was where Merv entertained his illustrious guests. The room was simple and elegant, but the view of the valley and rose garden was majestic.

I cooked dinner for our group that evening. We ate filet mignon served medium-to-well, just as Merv liked it, with a brown sauce and grilled onions, and potato au gratin, paired with a local Cabernet Sauvignon. For dessert, Annette served a traditional English trifle, which had been requested by Merv, who'd been told about it by Maggie.

We sat and ate together. Merv was a good man. He was good-spirited, kind, and complimentary. He told me he owned The Beverly Hilton Hotel and that, even though he was used to the finest meals, the food I'd made him outshone them by far. He enjoyed the trifle so much that he insisted on having a second portion.

Over the next week, Jack and Evelyn showed us the ropes. I listened carefully and began to compose a curriculum for the entire compound. At the end of the week, I presented the curriculum to Merv. Again, he was delighted.

Annette and I went back to Santa Monica to pack our belongings and returned two weeks later, when Jack and Evelyn were about to leave. During the day, I would typically tend to the grounds and then help Annette with the laundry. We made sure the house was clean and that Merv always had fresh sheets and towels.

During the week, Annette and I would have the compound to ourselves and every Friday, Saturday and Sunday, Merv and Tony would join us. I'd collect them at the airport in the station wagon on Friday evening and then Annette and I would tend to their needs for the weekend.

One weekend, Merv informed me that Zsa Zsa Gabor would be his guest for the evening. Gabor had been a Hollywood staple for years. The blonde bombshell was, although in her sixties at the time, always the talk of the celebrities. Born in Hungary, she and her sisters had arrived in the United States to become movie stars and socialites, just before the United States joined the allied forces of World War II in 1941. Zsa Zsa was the Hollywood favorite of her sisters after winning the title of Miss Hungary in 1936. She'd been married to the hotel magnate, Conrad Hilton, and now she would be visiting Merv Griffin. He wanted me to do "something special."

I began preparing for the meal as soon as Merv informed me. I polished the French crystal wine glasses and prepared a select grouping of roses from the rose garden. I laid the table with a pristine white linen tablecloth and arranged the roses in a beautiful bouquet that I placed in a clear crystal vase at the center of the table. The silver cutlery was polished so brightly you could see your face in it and it was arranged using a tape measure to ensure it was centered and symmetrical.

Merv and Zsa Zsa dined together, just the two of them. I served roast chicken stuffed with spinach and ricotta cheese topped with a light, lemon sauce. Sides of cauliflower and zucchini in brandy complimented the chicken, and for dessert, Annette had prepared a chocolate and raspberry soufflé. They both loved the meal. Zsa Zsa was the perfect guest. She was fun and her laugh was loud and infectious. They chatted with passion and a *joie de vivre* I had never seen before.

When Merv introduced me to Zsa Zsa, she asked me where I was from. Merv jumped up from the table and told her I was from the same place as the Beatles. She asked me if I'd ever met them and I told her that I hadn't, but I had visited their old stomping ground, The Cavern, on many occasions. Merv then told us all about the time he'd interviewed them on his show. I sat and listened along with Zsa Zsa, as if we were old friends.

Annette and I settled into our new lives. We renovated the rose garden and expanded it. We cooked British favorites for Merv and Tony every weekend. We'd serve them sausage rolls, Cornish pasties, steak and kidney pies, and Merv's favorite, Irish stew. Merv and Tony would be in bed by nine every evening, and in the mornings, I'd cook them bacon and eggs and serve it with freshly-squeezed orange juice.

In the afternoons, I'd drive Merv and Tony to the Carmel Tennis Club and leave them there to play tennis with their famous Hollywood friends. On the odd occasion, Merv and Tony would take Annette and me for lunch at The Monterey Fish Company.

One evening, Merv approached me to join him and Tony to watch television. He told me that Tony liked me and suggested that maybe we could have a threesome. This struck me as a terrible idea and eventually became one of the reasons I left Merv's employ.

I loved working for Merv but things began to get monotonous. The job was idyllic but it was anything but challenging. One day, I got a call from Dora at the agency. She had an opportunity for me to run a house in Beverly Hills. The client required silver service and a butler whose mission would be to pay attention to detail. This was my chance at realizing my dream of becoming a butler in Beverly Hills. I took the job on the condition that

Dora would inform Merv of the new arrangement. She agreed, but when Merv found out, I knew by just looking at him that he was disappointed. I told him I wouldn't leave until a suitable replacement had been found and trained and he seemed satisfied with the arrangement.

Sometime later, Merv invited me to be his guest for lunch at The Beverly Hilton Hotel. We sat and talked like old friends for hours. To this day, I miss him.

CHAPTER 24
THE GHOSTS OF ROXBURY DRIVE

Roxbury Drive was the home of the Hollywood stars of yesteryear. Stars such as Ginger Rogers, Jimmy Stewart and Peter Falk were just a few of the names who lived there in their twilight years.

My new assignment was for Mr. and Mrs. Feldstein, who lived in the 6,000 sq. ft. red brick mansion, once owned by the legendary comedian, Jack Benny The house had extensive, lush gardens, and a secluded swimming pool at the rear. This was my dream job. I'd been fixated on Beverly Hills since Elizabeth Taylor had suggested the location to me, after experiencing my elite level of service on board the Queen Elizabeth II cruise ship. Now I was here, waiting to be interviewed by the new inhabitant of the house, Mrs. Feldstein. She was a slight woman with light brown hair and a gaunt, ghost-like face, in her mid-forties. She was polite and welcomed me at the front door of the house, then took me to her office to be interviewed.

Her accent was hard to place. She told me she was English, but her accent was a strange mixture of generic American and Southern English. Right from the beginning, I knew she wanted to be treated like a queen. Mr. and Mrs. Feldstein were real estate magnates, who owned Mitsubishi Manufacturer's Bank, and their standards were way beyond the norm. She informed me that she and her husband had three children; David, who was seventeen, Michael, fifteen, and Sarah, twelve. My duties were to manage the house, with a cook and a maid to help. I was to take on the role of major domo, or house manager, and the duties were draconian, to say the least.

She read me a list of duties, of which the highest priority was given to evening silver service meals and floor-cleaning. I asked for an increase to my previous salary and she agreed without a beat. The job I always dreamed of was now mine.

Annette was once again working for Vista Real Estate and moved back into our apartment in Santa Monica. I lived with her on my days off, but during my work week, I lived in my own private apartment on the Feldstein property.

My first job was to polish the floors of the entire house. The silverware had to be polished and there was an entire living room filled with Tiffany lamps, each of which had to be polished in a daily rotation, along with the gigantic, crystal chandeliers. It was tough work, especially because each evening, I'd have to break away from my duties to set the table for a formal dinner and then perform silver service with white gloves, at Mrs. Feldstein's request.

She was a tough woman and I could tell her eyes were constantly on the prowl, searching for the slightest mistake. On the odd occasion, she would host over 200 people at the house for lavish parties, catered by Chasen's restaurant. The entertainment would consist of world-class musicians from New York and she would expect me to coordinate the whole thing. Her attitude made the household staff nervous wrecks, all except me. I'd trained myself to hide my severe anxiety well and I served her every day, without one complaint.

On the surface, to the outside world, the Feldsteins seemed to be the perfect family, but they were anything but perfect. One of the maids approached me in tears one day about the state of the rooms of the two boys. I inspected the rooms and was horrified to find that they'd spat on all the mirrors and literally trashed their rooms, knowing that the maid would have to clean up their mess. I calmed her down and told her I would clean it all up. When I eventually confronted them about it, they were cautiously defiant. I'd never seen behavior such as this before. Even the poor urchins I started life around wouldn't have behaved in such a way.

From the beginning of this new job, I began to feel unwell. The trauma of the past began to rear its head and I began to slowly lose myself and feel physically weak. I convinced the Feldsteins to allow me to take their exquisite blue Rolls Royce to be cleaned weekly and I used this time to get out of the house and drive around the neighborhood. It was the closest I got to therapy at the time.

One day, I was cleaning the pool area when I heard someone call from the house next door.

"Hello," said the soft female voice.

I looked over the wall and was amazed to see the Hollywood icon, Lucille Ball. I pretended not to know who she was.

"Who are you?" she asked.

"I'm Terry. Pleased to meet you."

She looked a little frustrated. "Terry, my maid's away for the day and I need to take the trash cans out. Will you help me?"

"Of course, I will, Lucy," I said as I began the short walk into her yard.

I took out her trash cans and then chatted with her for a few minutes. I ended the conversation by asking her if she needed a butler. She told me that her maid was enough, but I ended the conversation by telling her that, if she needed her trash cans taking out in the future, I'd gladly oblige if she'd make me a cup of tea as payment. Over the next few months, Lucy and I would have many cups of tea together and chat. Even though the years were showing, she was the same old Lucy, lovely to be around and a great source of comfort.

My health began to deteriorate further and, eventually, I made an appointment at Dr. Messina's office. After another gastrointestinal exam, he concluded that I was suffering once more from bleeding ulcers. Again, I had to go to his office weekly for shots of iron and I began to take medication to seal up the ulcers. We chatted again and he asked how things were. I told him of the stress I was experiencing at work and the fact that being on the run from Liverpool was mentally torturing me. He told me I had to mitigate my stress levels as much as possible. I decided then and there that I would hand in my resignation and leave the stress of the Feldstein residency.

During my final week with the Feldsteins, I was taking an afternoon walk in the neighborhood as I oftentimes did. It was the highlight of my day. The wide streets and the beautifully kept houses and gardens brought peace to my soul. On the way back one day, I noticed the great actor, Peter Falk, practicing his golf swing in his front yard. I stopped and introduced myself to him. He was the Feldsteins' next-door neighbor, but this was the first opportunity I'd had to meet him. He gave me a warm and gracious welcome and we chatted for a few minutes about golf. As I departed from the conversation, I marveled at the fact that I, the wanted bank robber from Liverpool, had been in conversation with the sharp-eyed television Detective Lieutenant Columbo and he was clueless about my true identity!

CHAPTER 25
FORTIFYING THE MIND AND BODY

I left the Feldsteins' employ and began to concentrate on getting my body and mind well again. I moved back in with Annette to the apartment in Santa Monica and began walking along the beach daily. The sea air, stress-free environment and walking was a start, but I knew I needed to test myself. Within a few short weeks, I was back at Mohammad Ali's gym. Jimmy Ellis was pleased to have me back. I'd go in for a few hours daily and jump rope, shadow box, do some bag work, and train with weights.

One day, I entered the gym and the whole place was set up by a representative for KO Magazine for a photo shoot with the world welterweight champion, Carlos Palomino. Carlos was a short, good-looking Mexican guy with a handlebar mustache. I told him I'd seen him fight Dave "Boy" Green in London. Instantly, we struck up a friendship.

I had my inversion boots with me and I asked him if he wanted to try them out. He agreed, so after fitting them to his ankles, I helped him to the high bar and watched him as he hung upside down, waiting for instructions. I told him to start with his arms hanging down toward the floor and then to reach up and touch his toes. Carlos grunted his way through twelve reps and then told me to get him down. He asked me how many I could do and I told him that I'd usually do four sets of 25, break and do some bag work, and then repeat the exercise twice more for a total of 300. He was astonished and asked me to show him.

When I finished, he turned to the KO Magazine representative and said, "Have you seen this guy? He's a superstar."

He told the guy to watch me train and suggested that the magazine do an article on me. Carlos and I became great friends.

Periodically, he'd take me to where he'd grown up in Westminster and we'd have coffee and chat for hours. He was waiting at the time to defend his title and I told him he might be fighting a member of my old, childhood gang, Ronnie Gibbons, who'd moved to New York years before and had become a contender.

I met and became friends with a few leading figures in the world of boxing. A few months after I resumed my training at the gym, legendary cut-man and coach of Mohammad Ali, Chuck Bodak, joined Jimmy Ellis to help him run the gym. Bodak introduced me to Sean O'Grady from Oklahoma. O'Grady was affectionately known as "The Bubblegum Kid" and was the light-weight champion of the world. I never missed an opportunity to train with the likes of Palomino and O'Grady, and slowly, I could feel myself gaining strength of body and clarity of mind.

One day, I got a call out of the blue. It was a friend of mine from Liverpool, Anto Garvey. Anto told me that a friend of his, a Liverpool boxer by the name of Brian Snaggs, wanted to come over to pursue his dream of being a professional boxer. I already knew of Brian. He was the Central Area Champion of Liverpool. I'd seen him fight and he was good.

Within two weeks, Brian had arrived on my doorstep. I took him to the gym, and after watching him work out, Chuck decided to train him for his first professional fight in the United States. After the training session, I asked Brian to try out the anti-gravity boots. He agreed and I helped him onto the high bar. He struggled to complete thirteen toe-touch sit-ups and then hung there helplessly. I laughed and he flipped. He got angry and told me to get him down. I did as he asked and tried my best to smooth the situation over, but Brian was a hothead.

Chuck suggested that Brian and I should take a drive to downtown Los Angeles and do some training at the Olympic Auditorium. He told us to introduce ourselves to Bobby Chacon, who at the time was the greatest Mexican fighter in the world.

We wasted no time. Brian and I were there the next day. The Olympic Auditorium had been built in 1924, and on the day it opened in 1925, Jack Dempsey and Rudolph Valentino were in attendance. It was a regular venue for both boxing and wrestling events and had been the site of the Olympics in 1932. When we arrived, the place looked degraded from the outside and the inner area looked no better. We walked in through a side door and the familiar smell of old sweat mixed with industrial detergent hit me in the face. The gym was well used with no frills and was similar to every quality, professional boxing gym I'd trained at.

A short, balding man with a small beard gave us a warm greeting. He was the coach there, Jimmy Montoya. We told him that Chuck had asked us to introduce ourselves to Bobby Chacon and it just so happened that Bobby was there at the time.

We explained Brian's situation to both, and without another word, Jimmy said, "Let's take a look at him."

Jimmy asked Brian to spar with a Mexican who'd had twenty-two fights and was close to the top of the tree. Brian agreed enthusiastically. It was war. Brian was aggressive and took it to the unsuspecting pro. Eventually, Jimmy had to end it. He told the two of them that this wasn't a fight, it was just sparring, but it was apparent to all that Jimmy was happy with what he'd seen. From then on Jimmy referred to Brian as "The Raging Bull."

We'd alternate training at the Olympic and Ali's gym. One day at the Olympic, a contender by the name of Brice Finch showed up. Brice had an upcoming fight against Sugar Ray Leonard and needed sparring partners. Brian didn't hesitate to volunteer. He went in hard and caught Brice with a left hook to the body, which dropped him immediately. Brice began to puke and sparring for him was over for the day.

Brian had a problem and that was his weight. He'd found work as a dishwasher in The Tudor House and just couldn't resist the food. The pastries and pies were his one vice. He was supposed to be a super-lightweight, fighting at 140 lbs. but, due to his eating habits, his weight would fluctuate between 140 and 150 lbs. constantly. This weight change would make him vacillate between Super Lightweight and Welterweight. Bobby Chacon didn't like this and it made it hard for Brian to get a fight.

We returned to Ali's gym and I concentrated my efforts on teaching Brian the method of training the mind and stomach that I'd developed while in Borstal, and later, in prison. After training just over six months in California, Brian became disillusioned because he couldn't get a fight and he returned to Liverpool to become the landlord of a local pub.

I'd now been happily unemployed for over six months, and because of all the training and rest between sessions, my ulcers had once again healed and I'd put on at least ten pounds of muscle.

Early one Monday morning, while lying in bed, my phone began to ring. I thought it must be someone in England so I rushed to answer it as soon as possible. It was Dora from the agency.

"Terry, where are you?" she said in her signature Italian accent. "You've been ignoring me. There are many clients who need an English butler. You have to come in today. I need to see you."

I could sense a desperation in her voice so I agreed to meet her in her office. When I got there, she sat me down and told me of a man in the Holmby Hills estate. He needed a butler to run his home. I listened as she laid out the specifics of the job. This man was single with no children, lived in a palatial house, and was away in Maryland for three weeks every month. He needed someone to secure the home, manage the house, assist his secretary, and on occasion, be his chauffeur. The job seemed like the ultimate low-maintenance gig. I wasn't interested in getting any more ulcers, so it seemed like the perfect fit for me.

Dora arranged an interview for me with the client on the upcoming Wednesday at two o'clock in the afternoon.

CHAPTER 26
FREDERICK WEISMAN THE
PHILANTHROPIC ART COLLECTOR

Frederick Weisman was a one-of-a-kind, the son of Russian Jews, who came to the United States to make a better life. He excelled in business as a young man and rose to the position of chairman of Hunts Foods by the time he was thirty-one. He formed a business alliance with a select group of Japanese businessmen, which led to the formation of Mid-Atlantic

Toyota, located in Maryland. It became the largest distributor of Toyota vehicles in the United States.

His altruistic endeavors were vast. He sponsored esteemed museums and art galleries and many charities that helped the impoverished and underprivileged. Although his name wasn't famous in the public realm, he was known and admired by the world's elites. Little did I know how my entrance into this man's life would affect me in the long-term.

I parked my Mustang right outside the massive wrought-iron gates and pressed the button on the intercom. A male voice came through the speaker.

"Hello," it said.

"Good afternoon, sir. This is Terry Moogan for Mr. Weisman."

"Come on in, Terry," replied the voice.

The gates slowly began to open. I parked the car, quickly brushed my gray suit down with my hands, and walked along the drive. The house was an exquisite Spanish-style colonial mansion. The large wooden door opened and there stood Mr. Frederick Weisman. He was short and slender, with dark, neatly combed hair and a pair of black, round-rimmed glasses. He was wearing a dark, pin-striped suit and a purple open-neck shirt. He introduced himself to me and shook my hand warmly.

"Dora told me everything about you," he said excitedly. "Let's go to my office."

He led me in through the front door and to the left, down a short hallway paved with glazed terracotta tile, and into his office. He walked behind his large, dark wood desk and held out his hand towards the guest chair.

I could tell by the manner of his dress and his neat, orderly desk that he was a man who paid attention to detail. He intricately explained what he required, and when I told him I would compose a curriculum for the house, he was impressed. With the job specifics over, he made small talk, asking me where I was from and what had brought me to California in the first place. I nodded and smiled as I answered, but inside, the anxiety was welling.

"I've wanted to come to California since Elizabeth Taylor told me all about it during my time serving her on the QEII," I said, but the real reason, of course, would have been far too shocking to disclose.

Finally, he stood and told me to follow him for a tour of the house. The relief hit me as Mr. Weisman instantly switched mode from interviewer to curator. He began in the kitchen and quickly led me through. He didn't know much about its various features, but just one look at it gave me the realization that this place would put the kitchens of most Michelin-star restaurants to shame.

He led me past the pool to the rose garden and down onto the tennis court. He then took me to my living quarters, overlooking the property of Barbara Streisand, who lived next door. I looked out from the window and imagined my workouts using the stone stairs for running and the tennis courts for shadow boxing and calisthenics.

When we got back to the main house, I asked him about his collection of artwork. He came alive and began giving me an in-depth historical analysis of each piece. His collection contained the works of Bacon and Warhol, to name but a few. He asked me if I would periodically help him move the artwork. It was then that I knew I had the job.

"I'd be delighted," I replied.

We walked into the living room and the first thing I noticed was the large white grand piano.

"Do you play the piano, Mr. Weisman?"

"No," he said with a wry smile. "I just collect art."

We stood for a few seconds facing the large windows leading out to the grounds. It was five acres of land with every square foot in use. I saw the pride in his gaze.

"I'm only here for ten days a month," he said. "The rest of the time, I'll be in Maryland at the headquarters of Toyota in the United States."

He then began to walk, so I followed closely behind him. The garage was the next port of call. To the right, facing the garage door, was a black, one-of-a-kind Toyota sports car, which had been featured in the James Bond movie, "You Only Live Twice." Right next to it was a sky-blue, 1973 Corniche Rolls Royce.

He led me out through the garage doors and back into the house. We descended the stairs into the wine cellar. His collection was vast. He told me that his secretary ordered all the wines, most of which came from Europe. We walked along a wall racked with what appeared to be thousands of bottles of wine, and eventually, we arrived at his private subterranean office. The walls were covered with diplomas, certificates and photos.

He once again sat me down, looked me straight in the eye and said, "When do you want to start?"

"Monday," I said without hesitation, "so if it's alright with you, Mr. Weisman, I'll move in on Sunday evening."

He nodded and held out his hand. I shook it and he led me out of the house.

I arrived the next Sunday with my luggage. Mr. Weisman gave me the key code for the back gate. I unpacked my bags and prepared my uniform for the next day; a starched white shirt, pressed black pants, and a black tie. He told me what he wanted for breakfast and the time he wanted it served and left me to settle in.

I called Annette. We were obviously living apart again, but this time, I was only a short drive away, so the separation wasn't that much of a big deal. I described my living quarters and gave her a detailed description of the grounds. It was to be my first day the next morning and my anxiety was heightened. Speaking with her and listening to her soft, reassuring voice calmed me.

I woke up on Monday morning at exactly 5.30 am. Mr. Weisman had told me he would be arriving at the dining room table at 5.55 am. I arrived in the kitchen at 5.40 am. His orange juice and milk were in the refrigerator. I decanted both into matching carafes and placed them in the refrigerator to keep them cold. I filled a small cereal bowl with raisin bran and placed it before his seat at the table. I waited, and at exactly 5.55 am, I heard the repetitive click of the leather soles of his shoes tapping on the floor. The clicking got louder until his frame appeared at the table.

"Good morning, Mr. Weisman," I said, trying not to sound too nervous.

"Good morning, Terry."

He was wearing a perfectly-tailored, gray, three-piece suit, a red and white plaid shirt, and a silk, multi-colored tie. He sat at the table, and as the air was disrupted around him, the smell of his cologne, Aramis, wafted into my nose. I placed the orange juice and milk on the table and poured him an eight-ounce glass of orange juice from the carafe.

"I'll only be ten minutes, Terry," he said as he glanced at his gold Piaget watch.

He then poured milk on the cereal and began to eat. I retired to the kitchen and began my chores for the day. When his bowl was empty, he popped his head into the kitchen and said, "Terry, I'm done. I'll be downstairs in my office."

That first day, after I finished cleaning up Mr. Weisman's breakfast, I concentrated on the master bedroom. I cleaned the green Italian marble bathroom, replaced the sheets on his four-poster, king-sized bed and then spent the rest of the day getting to know the house and composing the curriculum.

I concentrated on memorizing his habits. Every day, he would leave the house for lunch at precisely midday, driving his Rolls Royce to one of his three favorite lunch-time restaurants: Chasen's, Trader Vic's, or The Polo Lounge. To facilitate the process, I would prepare the car, driving it to the front door, and leaving the engine running. In the evenings, he would go out for dinner, so I would repeat the process with the car.

During the day, I would gather roses from the garden and arrange them in bouquets to place in the center of the many tables in the house. I would clean the floors, silverware, and chandeliers. On one occasion, Mr. Weisman commented on how clean the chandeliers were and asked how I cleaned them. I informed him that I first had to strip them down and then clean them with hot water and vinegar.

Although Mr. Weisman was cordial, he was busy and it seemed that he rarely had the time to chat. My work around the house was enjoyable, but it took so much of my time that I was spending next to no time with Annette. I knew she was an excellent cook, so I came up with the idea of asking Mr. Weisman if Annette and I could work for him as a team. Annette would take care of the kitchen, while I would take care of the day-to-day cleaning schedule and the general day-to-day running of the house.

I thought that Mr. Weisman would resist the idea and thought of it as nothing more than a wishful idea, but when I approached him in his office and asked him, he simply turned his head in my direction, looked up into the air for a few seconds in thought and then nodded and said, "Yes, that's a good idea, Terry." Within the week, Annette had once again handed in her notice at the real estate agents, and within no time, she had moved in with me.

Mr. Weisman loved Annette. He'd make a point of chatting to her, complementing her, and loved the food she made him. Well, not all the food. Since Annette had begun working for Mr.

Weisman, he'd begun staying at home for lunch. One day, Annette decided to serve him tinned salmon mixed with mayonnaise. It was the one time I saw him upset. As youths in Liverpool, any salmon, even tinned salmon, was considered a luxury, but this was not the case when it came to a man of the caliber of Mr. Weisman. He flung his arms in the air.

"Get this away from me!" he said. "Don't ever serve something like this to me again."

Annette was embarrassed and asked if she could make him something else. He shook his head ferociously and screamed, "Terry, I'm going out for lunch." I asked him if I could drive him to make up for the mistake. He agreed.

When we arrived at Trader Vic's, Mr. Weisman said, "Leave the car here, Terry, you're coming with me."

Mr. Weisman and I left the car at the valet stand and walked toward the Beverly Hilton Hotel and into the prestigious annex restaurant, the regular haunt of notable Hollywood legends like Frank Sinatra and his melodious gang, The Rat Pack. The Captain seated us at Mr. Weisman's regular table, overlooking the pool.

We sat and spoke like old friends. He once again told me about his art collection and explained to me that the works in the house were only a fraction of the pieces he owned. He seemed to be inspired and told me that, the next morning, we'd be changing around the positions of the art in the house. He apologized for the way he reacted towards Annette and told me he would send her to culinary school to learn the finer points of cooking.

CHAPTER 27
OLD BLACK EYES

The following Sunday, Mr. Weisman departed for Maryland. I drove him to Los Angeles Airport, and just before we arrived, he told me that during his time away he'd be having a brand new, racing-green Bentley delivered to the house. Before he got out of the car, he advised me that he wanted me to pick him up curbside when he returned and informed me that he'd call me at the house a few days before leaving Maryland with further instructions.

I arrived back at the house less than an hour later. We had the place to ourselves now. I told Annette to get ready to go out for a drive. We cruised through the Hollywood Hills in the Rolls Royce and took in the breathtaking scenery. We stopped off at Gelson's luxury grocery store in Century City and bought some of the best produce to practice recipes for when Mr. Weisman returned.

A few days passed and the new car arrived. I examined it with the delivery driver. It was perfect. It was the only one of its kind in the United States. That night, I told Annette we were going for a drive. We took our places on the Bentley's soft, beige leather, and deeply inhaled the smell of leather and luxury. We drove to Santa Monica and parked right outside the mock Tudor building of The Olde King's Head Pub. Everyone was staring at us as we exited the car. We sat on the patio and gazed at the people who'd stopped just to look at the magnificent machine.

Here I was, a twenty-six-year-old man on the run, sitting in a pub in Santa Monica, driving a luxury car, and in charge of a $30 million house in Hollywood Hills. The Social Services in Liverpool could never picture me living the life I was living. It felt surreal, and in that moment, it felt good, but the anxiety of being on the run was still crushing me internally. After dinner, Annette and I drove up Santa Monica Boulevard and back to Holmby Hills. It had been a wonderful evening.

Mr. Weisman arrived back on a Sunday evening. I met him curbside in the Bentley, as he'd instructed. He looked like a child on Christmas morning when he saw the car.

"Isn't it marvelous, Terry?"

He ran around, inspecting it from the hood to the trunk. I opened the rear door for him, but he opened the front passenger door himself and rode shotgun. As we pulled away from the curb, I reached into the cassette rack and grabbed a cassette tape.

"Look, Mr. Weisman, they left a tape for you to enjoy."

I pushed the tape into the machine and Frank Sinatra's "My Way" began gently playing through the speakers. Mr. Weisman exploded. He pushed the eject button on the cassette machine, and when the tape popped out, he grabbed it and threw it out of the side window of the car.

"I don't want to hear that motherfucker!" he screamed, "And that prick Dean Martin can go and fuck himself too!"

I was absolutely gob-smacked. "I'm so sorry, Mr. Weisman. I had no idea you didn't like him."

He calmed down and shook his head. "I'm hungry, Terry. Take me to Trader Vic's."

We parked at the valet stand and he once again requested that I join him for the meal. We sat and the mood was still tense. I waited for him to start a conversation, hoping he would tell me about the contention between himself and "Old Blue Eyes."

We ate and made small talk throughout the dinner. When we finally finished, he waited for the waiter to take our plates and said, "I suppose you want to know why I feel the way I do about Sinatra?"

I shrugged in an effort to appear disinterested. Mr. Weisman smirked at my response.

"Many years ago, I was in The Polo Lounge with a date. I wanted things to be romantic, but it just so happened that it was

Dean Martin's birthday and The Rat Pack were partying there to celebrate. Things were getting a little rowdy. I shouted at them to be quiet and Sinatra pointed at me and said something along the lines of, 'Shut your mouth, you four-eyed little Jew!'

"I couldn't control myself, Terry. I jumped out of my seat and punched him off his chair. My fist landed perfectly on his nose. I saw his eyes beginning to close, but I was pissed so I followed him down to the floor to punch him a few more times. The next thing I know, I was waking up in the hospital with a subdural hematoma. Apparently, when I reached down to give old Frankie a further beating, one of his goons hit me on the head with what's thought to be a telephone."

I sat there in disbelief.

"I'm glad you work for me, Terry," he continued. "I've seen you working out and I know you're a decent boxer and can take care of yourself. I want you to drive for me more often from now on, because I can sometimes get out of line. I need someone like you to keep an eye out for me. I'm sure Sinatra's still pissed at me about that incident. I embarrassed him in front of his friends and guys like him can wait a long time to get their own back. He's connected, Terry, understand?"

My Liverpool sense of humor couldn't let a moment like this go to waste.

"Yes, Mr. Weisman, I understand, and I'm impressed. You've got balls. I can't believe you turned Old Blue Eyes into Old Black Eyes."

We both laughed so hard that patrons at other tables stopped their conversations and stared at us. All this time, unbeknownst to me, I'd been both my boss' butler and his bodyguard.

CHAPTER 28
THE GREAT PICASSO

Mr. Weisman rarely talked to me over breakfast. He was a man of discipline and habit. His usual routine, the only routine I'd witnessed, was for him to arrive at the breakfast table at precisely six o'clock in the morning, immediately eat his standard bowl of raisin bran, drink his orange juice, and then descend to his office under the house.

There was only one day I witnessed him changing his breakfast habit. It was a Wednesday morning in the spring. Usually, I could hear the leather soles of his shoes tapping on the floor as he made his way to the dining room, but this time, the cadence of the taps was faster and lighter. He sat at the table and turned toward me.

"Terry, I need to talk to you," he said. "We're having a new piece delivered today. It should be here by two o'clock. Oh, and I'm going out for lunch today. Have the Corniche ready for me on the front drive at noon."

I nodded. "Very good, Mr. Weisman."

He ate his breakfast and then scurried off to his subterranean office. I cleaned up the breakfast dishes and then continued with the general chores of the house. At midday, after I positioned the vehicle, he burst through the front door and replaced me in the driver's seat.

"Remember, Terry, the new piece is arriving at two. Get them to leave it in the living room," he said excitedly before he drove off.

"Will do," I said as I walked off back into the house.

At approximately 1.30 pm, a large van arrived at the front gate. The driver buzzed the intercom.

"Delivery for Mr. Weisman," he said.

I pushed the button and the van slowly edged into the driveway. The driver and his helper jumped out and opened the roller-door at the back. The helper climbed in and prepared a pallet jack as the driver pulled the ramp out of its compartment and lowered it gently to the floor. A few seconds went by and the helper pushed a small crate out of the back of the van and onto the pallet jack. He struggled as he pushed it down the ramp and into the house. The driver followed him with a small crowbar in his hand.

I pointed to the living room and the two of them placed the crate in the center. As soon as the man pulled the pallet jack from under the crate, the driver got to work pulling the crate apart with the crowbar. Pieces of wood were being discarded by the second until the entire crate was destroyed. What was left was a cardboard box with an official-looking seal surrounding it. I left it propped against a wall as the driver and his helper cleared up the mess and returned to the van.

At just after two o'clock, Mr. Weisman returned. He ran from the car and slammed through the front door.

"Is it here, Terry? Did it arrive?" he asked, like a child on Christmas morning.

"Yes, Mr. Weisman, it's in the living room," I said.

He ran into the living room and I followed him in with great anticipation. He looked at the box in silence for a few moments and then turned to me.

"Open it up," he said tersely.

I did as he asked. I fiddled with the tamper-proof seal and had to reach into my pocket for my folding knife. In a few short seconds, the seal was off and the box was open. I pulled out the canvas that was inside and propped it against the wall, where the box had previously stood.

Mr. Weisman was fixated on the painting. It seemed as though he was hypnotized by it. I'd never seen him like this before. I watched him in the same way he was watching the painting.

"Mother and Child," he said, without taking his eyes off the piece.

"It's beautiful," I replied.

"This is one of Picasso's greatest masterpieces," he said. "It's one of a series of Madonnas, created during his Blue Period. It was completed by the master himself in 1901. Will you hang it for me please, Terry?"

"Of course."

I jogged out of the house and into the garage to retrieve a hammer, a tape measure and a few nails, then jogged back.

"Where should it go?" he asked.

I scanned the room for a few seconds and then pointed to the space over the fireplace.

"It needs to go there," I said. "She can watch over the house and protect us."

Mr. Weisman nodded. "Ok, Terry."

I grabbed a chair and measured the wall horizontally over the fireplace. I placed a nail in the center line of the wall and gently tapped it in with the hammer. I then hung the Madonna. I replaced the chair and stood at the side of the room to watch his reaction. He slowly walked to each corner of the room and viewed the piece from every angle. Eventually, his gaze turned towards me for approval.

"It's beautiful," I said.

He smiled and nodded, then continued to gaze at the masterpiece.

It was at that time that I truly began to appreciate the art in Mr. Weisman's home. From Giacomo Manzu's full-sized, pure white sculpture, 'Grande Cardinale,' placed in front of the arched windows, facing inwards to seemingly bless the house, to the exquisite Francis Bacon brightly-colored originals in the living room and along the walls of the stairs, the whole place took on a new, vibrant dimension to me.

I could tell that our relationship was beginning to change. Mr. Weisman opened up to me and began asking for my opinion. One day, I'd just collected the newspaper from the front doorstep when I noticed him walking down the stairs wearing a purple, black-spotted sweater. I'd never seen him in anything other than a suit before, so this was a strange sight to me. When our eyes met, he stopped in the middle of the staircase and pointed to the sweater with his hands.

"What do you think?"

"You look like a jockey," I responded.

Without another word, he turned and ran back up the stairs. A few minutes later, he came back down the stairs, wearing a plain, white sweater. He approached me and told me the purple sweater had been a gift from the Norton and Simon art gallery. He mentioned that he'd previously been married to the owner's sister and that they'd probably given him the sweater to make him look stupid. I later found the sweater in a trash can in Mr. Weisman's personal bathroom.

During this time, I walked into the office one day to clean. An insurance adjuster had been by, and under a paperweight, was a sheet showing the insurance value for the Picasso. It was for $75 million. The thought instantly went through my head that I should call Ronnie Gibbons and tell him to come and steal the painting. But then, I remembered that word, Redemption, and knew I was now a better man than that.

CHAPTER 29
THE PRESIDENT AND THE PLANE

Summers were always full of surprises. One beautiful summer day, Mr. Weisman sat down for breakfast as he always did. He ate, and as he stood to leave, he looked back at me.

"There'll be two black cars coming to the house today. As soon as they arrive, let them in, Terry."

"Yes, Mr. Weisman," I said before he disappeared down into his office.

Not more than an hour later, I heard the intercom buzz beside the front gate. I looked out to see the two black cars Mr. Weisman had described. I pressed the button to open the gate and the two cars drove slowly onto the driveway. I stood at the front door to welcome the mysterious visitors. The back door of the first car opened and the President of the United States, Ronald Reagan himself, stepped out.

"Good morning, Sir," I said.

He walked towards me, shook my hand and smiled warmly. "Good morning,' he said. "My daughter's here to play tennis with some of my agents."

His daughter, Patty, got out of the car, along with a group of three other Secret Service Agents, all wearing tennis attire. They walked around the house, past the pool, down the stairs and onto the tennis courts.

The President smiled at me and got back into the car. Both vehicles drove slowly out of the driveway. Patty and the agents played for a few hours. I made lunch for them and brought drinks and was on hand constantly, making sure their drinking water was replenished.

They returned many times to play and both Mr. Weisman and

I were happy to host them. A few weeks after our first meeting, President Reagan returned unannounced. I greeted him at the front door. He reached into the car and pulled out a framed, signed photo of himself. He handed it to me and asked me to give it to Mr. Weisman. That was the last time I saw him.

One morning after breakfast, the boss asked me to get the car ready. I asked him which car he wanted to use. He seemed stressed by the decision. He stood in front of me, shaking his head.

"We have to go to the airport, Terry. I can't make up my mind. You decide."

"Ok, we'll take the Corniche," I said.

He seemed relieved by my decision. I prepared the car and drove it to the front door. Mr. Weisman got into the front passenger seat.

"We have to drive to Van Nuys Airport, Terry. I'm going to buy a plane. I'm sick and tired of commercial flights."

I could tell by his tone of voice that he was excited. It was a similar excitement to when the Picasso arrived.

We drove through the valley and onto the grounds of the airport, where Mr. Weisman directed me to a large hangar. I parked the car and we walked inside the structure. There, in front of us, was a beautiful, navy-blue Gulfstream IV jet. There were four men in suits standing next to it. Two of the men were introduced as pilots and the other two were obviously salesmen. After they introduced themselves, Mr. Weisman cut straight to the chase.

"I'm going on a test flight, Terry. Want to come?"

"No thanks, Mr. Weisman," I replied. "I'll wait here with the car."

"Nonsense. You're coming along for the ride," he said.

We boarded the plane. The pilots told us we'd be taking off in 20 minutes. I looked around the cabin. There were 12 large, comfortable, beige leather seats, a spacious center aisle, and the walls and ceiling were covered in dark, varnished wood. A beautiful, slim, dark-haired flight attendant in business attire offered us drinks and snacks after take-off.

"Do you like it, Terry?" asked Mr. Weisman.

"Yes, sir, I do."

After about an hour, we landed. Mr. Weisman asked the four men to join him at the house. They obliged, and when we got back home, he asked me to take the two pilots out for a drink. The salesmen, who had driven their own car to the house, stayed with Mr. Weisman to complete the purchase of the plane. I told him I'd take the pilots to dinner in the Bentley. He handed me a credit card and waved us on our way.

We went to the King's Head in Santa Monica. We drank Guinness and ate steak and kidney pies. The pilots told me that, if Mr. Weisman bought the plane, they would be his personal pilots. The asked me about him, his habits, his personality and his temperament. I told them the truth: that he was fair, timely, and disciplined, but if things went wrong, he could get upset. We arrived back at the house a few hours later and the salesman were finishing up the paperwork. The pilots and the salesmen left together after a few minutes. I looked for Mr. Weisman and found him in the living room.

"Did you buy yourself a plane?"

"Yes, Terry, I did," he replied with a smile.

Mr. Weisman commissioned the artist, Ed Rushe, to paint the plane a darker shade of blue, with white stars interspersed all over it, so it would blend in with the night sky when he flew to New York and Maryland during the night. Rushe painted the cabin ceiling sky blue with white clouds, so the view would blend in with the ceiling during daytime flights. The plane became one of Mr. Weisman's most prized possessions.

CHAPTER 30
SOME THINGS CHANGE,
SOME THINGS STAY THE SAME

Mr. Weisman was conscious about his weight. He would record his measurements regularly, and every once in a while, he'd visit The Golden Door in Escondido for a week. The Golden Door was a luxury health spa catering to the rich and famous. Many would go there as a refuge to decompress and lose weight, while eating the healthiest and tastiest foods available.

Each time he went, he'd have Annette and me drive him there. We'd drop him off and then return through Laguna Beach and some of the other beach cities of Southern California. We'd stop for lunch on the way back and sometimes check into a hotel for the evening before returning to the house. When we'd pick him up after a week, he'd always be at least 15 lbs. lighter.

Mr. Weisman loved the food served at The Golden Door, so he paid the head chef there to come to the house and teach Annette and me his culinary magic. We used the skills the chef taught us to serve many of the world's elites at Mr. Weisman's house. They included the directors of Toyota from Japan, bankers, art dealers, and members of the prestigious Rothschild family.

One of the highlights of my day was collecting the mail from Mr. Weisman's mailbox in West Hollywood. I'd drive the Corniche and take my time, savoring the views and reveling in the fact that random people would stop and stare at the car as I drove by.

One day, I stopped at a red traffic light on Lexington Avenue. Right next to me was a yellow Rolls Royce Corniche, almost identical to the model I was driving. I looked over at the driver and he caught my eye. It was the legendary actor, Michael Caine.

"Good morning, Michael. Not bad for a scouser, eh?" I shouted.

He laughed and waved at me as the light turned green. We drove off in different directions.

The Weisman household was orderly, and due to his disciplined mentality, my boss rarely made mistakes. One day, I was cleaning up his bedroom and I walked through a storage room between his room and the guest room. There was a safe in the room that was usually closed, but this time, it was wide open. I inspected the contents. There were two cloth bags. At first glance, when I took them from the safe, it appeared that one of them was filled with approximately $30,000 in cash and the other one was filled with about $250,000 worth of jewelry.

At that moment, I looked back on my life. When I was living in Liverpool, struggling to survive, I would've taken this loot in an instant, but I'd changed. I'd become a better man. I trusted Mr. Weisman and respected him immensely. I placed both bags back in the safe and secured it. The next morning, I informed his secretary about the unsecured safe.

Mr. Weisman began spending more time in both Maryland and New York. It almost broke my heart the day his secretary told me that he would be hiring a part-time cleaner for the house and he would no longer need the services of myself and Annette. I had been in Mr. Weisman's employ for just under three years and it had been the best education I'd had in the United States up to that time. I was so grateful to him for the opportunity.

The house eventually became a museum, due to the trust Mr. Weisman set up for after his death. In 2018, I booked a tour of the house with my daughter, Kelly. When we arrived, I was shocked to see that the house was exactly the same as it had been when I worked there. There were about six people on the tour and when Louise, the tour guide, saw me, she asked me to introduce myself to the rest of the group. I realized during that first visit back how special it was to have been Mr. Weisman's butler. The house felt to me like I'd never left. Periodically, I go back to visit, to reminisce, and remember the good old days.

CHAPTER 31
THE WEINBERG TRAGEDY

Dora was surprised at the news that Mr. Weisman had let us go. We arranged to meet at her office on a Monday morning to discuss my next career move. When I got there, she already had a position to offer me. It was a job for an extremely wealthy and influential couple, Mr. and Mrs. Weinberg.

William Weinberg was a real estate investor, who had bought the Kahala Hilton Hotel in the late 1970s and decided to manage it himself. The hotel was the vacation destination of the world's celebrities and high rollers. As a result, he only resided in his home in the Trousdale Estates in Beverly Hills for approximately one week of every month.

But Dora informed me that the job would be tough. The job offer was for the position of major domo, the house manager, and as such, I would oversee a chef, as well as a husband-and-wife team, comprised of a butler and a maid. Dora told me that the only person who needed service in the house daily was William Weinberg's wife, Nancy, and that she could be "difficult."

I arrived at the Weinberg's house on the Wednesday after my meeting with Dora at her agency. Doris, Mr. Weinberg's secretary, interviewed me for the position. She seemed impressed by my resume. She emphasized how demanding Mrs. Weinberg could be and seemed to dwell on the issue, which made me quite nervous. But then, after all, she was only one person in the gigantic and opulent house. I told myself not to worry.

The interview was more than an hour long, and at the end, Doris shook my hand. I didn't know whether the job was mine or not until Doris scheduled a second interview for me later in the week. On arrival, I was met by her big smile. She seemed more relaxed around me this time and took the time to give me a tour of the house.

She explained that it had once been the residence of Elvis Presley and was set on three acres of land, with cabanas around the pool, tennis courts, and lavish gardens. She showed me the annex adjoining the garage and informed me that it would be my living quarters. Annette and I had already moved back into our Santa Monica apartment, so once again, I would live at my client's house and meet up with Annette on my days off.

I told her I could write a curriculum for the house, in order to ensure smooth day-to-day running of the household and she seemed thrilled. I met Paul, the chef, and the husband-and-wife domestic couple, Jeff and Linda, but I found it odd that I was yet to meet Mrs. Weinberg.

Jeff and Linda were a good team and ran the house autonomously. They understood and followed my curriculum without any problems. Paul, however, was a nervous wreck. He was small and polite and quite obviously effeminate. From the first day, it was evident that Mrs. Weinberg hated Paul. She would stay in her room and have her meals brought to her by Linda, but I could hear her screaming as her food was delivered.

"This is shit!" she would shout, along with a series of other diatribes, usually focused on Paul.

After the second day, Doris told me that Nancy wanted to meet me. She took me to her bedroom and introduced us. From the moment I saw her, I knew she was mentally ill. She was short and emaciated with long red hair and pale, almost translucent skin. Her face was gaunt and the sockets of her eyes were surrounded by almost purple skin. Although she was in her early forties, she looked much older. She wore a mauve nightgown and lay on the bed as she made conversation with me. She was polite, a far cry from the screaming banshee I'd heard during the previous day.

Nancy told me she would like me to deliver her meals from now on and I obviously agreed. She moved between her bedroom and the kitchen and didn't seem to go elsewhere in the house.

In the evenings, I'd hear her slamming around in the kitchen, complaining that the fridge wasn't stocked the way she wanted it to be.

I would deliver three meals a day to her in her room. The journey to her room from the kitchen was eerie. The corridors reminded me of the movie, "The Shining." They were long, dimly lit, and gloomy. The days of Elvis and his lavish, lively parties were long gone.

"Do you like the food today, Mrs. Weinberg?" I'd say.

"It's fucking shit," she'd routinely reply. "I know he's gay," she'd remark, referring to the chef.

Mr. Weinberg arrived during my second week of employment. I expected him to be like his wife, but he was a lovely man. He expected his food to be formally served to him and he was always grateful. The first time I served him, I had the chef make him lamb chops with asparagus and potatoes, followed by English trifle. He seemed delighted. Mr. Weinberg didn't stay long, though, and during my many months working in the household, he came home less and less frequently.

The relationship between Paul and Mrs. Weinberg was heartbreaking and difficult to observe. She bullied him relentlessly. It was constant. There was no getting away from her. He was literally held captive.

Early in the morning at around 4 am one day, I woke up to a sound like a car engine. I turned on the light and noticed what appeared to be smoke billowing from the vents in the room. I dressed quickly and ran into the garage, thinking that there was a fire. What I found was one of the most disturbing sights I'd ever seen.

Mrs. Weinberg was sitting in the passenger seat of her Rolls Royce. A hose was connected to the exhaust by one end and the other end was hanging out of her mouth. She was unconscious. I ran and opened the door of the garage, turned off the ignition, and dragged her out onto the floor. I called for an ambulance, and within minutes, the police and an ambulance arrived. The police took a statement from me as the paramedics hoisted her onto a gurney and administered oxygen.

One of the paramedics asked me how old she was and when I answered, "I think she's forty-three," she pulled off her mask and shouted, "Forty-four."

For the next few days, Mrs. Weinberg would call from Cedars Sinai hospital and say, "What's for dinner tonight?"

Every day, Paul would make the food and I would deliver it to her. Her attempted suicide was the last straw for the staff. A meeting was held and Paul, Jeff and Linda decided to quit. Doris was mortified. She begged me to stay and told me that Mrs. Weinberg was sick and needed me. I did as she asked. I stayed. Now it was just predominantly Nancy and me in the house.

She began requesting food from Nate and Al's, a nearby deli. I'd place her meal on a plate on a silver tray and walk it up that dark hallway. Our conversations changed from her critiquing the food to her telling me about her personal and psychological problems. I'd been anxious and stressed since the horrors of my childhood, but I'd learned to suppress those feelings. But now, being in this house with this woman brought it all back. I had to stay calm and measured, in order to keep her somewhat grounded and this just added to my own mental torment. I called Dora and told her about the situation. She asked me to "hang in there" and sympathized, but there was nothing else she could do.

A few days afterwards, I ordered a plate of salmon and lox from Nate and Al's for Mrs. Weinberg's dinner. She'd been quiet all day and had left me alone after lunch, which was not unusual. When the food arrived, I prepared it as I usually did and placed it on the silver tray, along with a bowl of fresh strawberries, accompanied with chocolate sauce.

At 6 o'clock in the evening, I began to walk along the corridor towards her room, when I heard a deafening bang. I stopped in my tracks and stood motionless as the realization of what had just happened hit me. I turned around on the spot, took the tray back to the kitchen, and called emergency services.

An ambulance arrived, with the police not far behind. I saw them get to work. They chatted while preparing equipment and engaging in their work. It was just business to them. I gave the police a statement and left the house, only to return to collect my things from my living quarters.

A few days after Mrs. Weinberg's tragic death, in May 1984, Dora called to tell me that Mr. Weinberg had called her to request that I meet him in Hawaii. Annette and I met him at his hotel, which was located on a pristine, white beach on the island of Oahu.

He paid for our flights, accommodation, and meals and joined us for dinner in the evenings during our ten-day stay. He was a generous gentleman. He was easy to talk to and seemed to be at peace. On our last night, Mr. Weinberg took me aside to speak to me in private. During the conversation, he asked for my discretion in reference to his wife's death. I gave him my assurances and kept my word. At the time of writing this memoir, it's been eleven years since William Weinberg's death, and as such, I believe that an appropriate amount of time has passed to allow me to tell this tragic story.

CHAPTER 32
THE MAKEUP MOGUL

I called Dora immediately on our return from Hawaii and asked her if there were any positions available. I was worried about the future. The Weinberg job had increased my anxiety level and I knew that another job as emotionally draining as it had been might just be the end of me.

What came next out of Dora's mouth was exactly what I needed to hear.

"Terry, you've had some tough positions. There's one available for one man living in Holmby Hills. It might just be what both he and you need right now."

The client was Davis Factor, son of Max Factor, the iconic makeup tycoon. Max Factor had been born in Poland in the late 19th century. His father, a textile worker, couldn't afford to send his four children to school, so by the time David was eight, he began working as an assistant to a pharmacist. At the age of nine, he began an apprenticeship with a wig-maker, which in turn gave him the experience to work at a famous hairstylist, Anton's.

Upon his discharge from his compulsory service in the Imperial Russian Army, David opened his own shop in the town of Ryazan in Western Russia. He began supplying cosmetics and perfumes to the royal family, which led to him being monitored more closely. He got married and he and his wife, Esther Rosa, had three children, Freda, Cecillia, and Davis.

Due to the rise of anti-Semitism, the Factor family left Russia covertly and arrived at Ellis Island at the beginning of 1904. They settled in St. Louis, Missouri, but after the tragic death of his wife, Esther Rosa, shortly after giving birth to their fourth child, Frank, David moved to Los Angeles with his children. He began supplying wigs and makeup for the up-and-coming movie industry. After his death in 1938, his children took the reins and eventually sold the business to Beatrice Foods, making them collectively billionaires.

My interview with Davis Factor took place on the following Monday, after I met with Dora. It was scheduled for 2 pm. I arrived at the gates of the magnificent stone building ten minutes early, giving me just enough time to scan the beautiful gardens as I drove slowly along the driveway.

Barbara Bentley, Mr. Factor's daughter, met me at the front door. She was a short, slim woman in her mid-forties. She was dressed in a navy-blue skirt and matching jacket, giving her the appearance of a business executive. I could tell instantly that she was a taskmaster and would prove to be extremely protective of her father, Davis Factor.

She walked me into an elegant drawing room and introduced me to Mr. Factor. Davis was well into his seventies at the time. He was slim and looked frail, with thinning, white hair, dark-rimmed glasses, and bony facial features. But he was polite, softly spoken, and seemed kind.

Barbara did most of the talking. She asked me about my experiences and listened as I told her how I'd set up a dining room for a formal party of twelve. I thought about the irony of it all. These people had known nothing but wealth and opulence their whole lives and here was I, a former street urchin from the toughest, inner-city area of Liverpool, telling them how to present their home to visiting guests.

The interview lasted for over ninety minutes. Barbara informed me that her father had two nurses, each of whom took care of him for 12-hour shifts and that I'd be required to drive and tend to him as part of my duties. Davis began talking about the Max Factor empire and gave me a brief history.

When the meeting ended, although Barbara and Davis seemed happy with me, they didn't tell me if I had the job or not. The reason for this was that Dora had another British butler to interview for the job. John Hammond was an experienced butler from Leeds. While I was interviewing for the job of Mr. Factor's butler, John was interviewing for a similar position with "Lethal Weapon" movie director, Richard Donner. I'd met John in Dora's office and we'd decided that we would both interview for the two jobs and then let the clients determine the best fit.

A couple of days after my first Factor interview, I arrived at the house for a second interview. This time, Davis and Barbara took me on a tour of the house. It was flanking the immaculately-kept Arm and Hammer Park. We looked out from the living room at the large swimming pool and the multi-colored, visually over-loaded rose garden. Barbara then took me to a large second-floor room overlooking the grounds that I'd be allocated as my living quarters.

When the tour was over, they offered me the job. It was just what I needed at the time. I would serve Davis his breakfast, consisting of an orange, a slice of toast, raisin bran, and, of course, coffee at eight o'clock every morning. I would perform various duties around the house and then, at approximately 1 pm, Davis, his nurse, and I would go to Malibu for lunch and walk through The Colony, the stylish shopping district next to Pepperdine College. In the evenings, I would sometimes cook him a light meal or we would go out to a local restaurant.

Every week, I'd take him to his stockbrokers in Century City, where he'd buy two million dollars' worth of stocks. The stock wasn't real, though. Barbara knew that her father had a compulsion for buying stocks, so she convinced the stockbroker to humor him during his visits.

Barbara lived close by, on the prestigious Lindon Drive. She'd constantly ask me, "How's he doing?" and I'd constantly reply that he was doing just fine, urging her not to worry.

The nurses were always nervous when Barbara was around. She was demanding and unapproachable. I noticed that every once in a while, Barbara would smoke by herself in the courtyard. One day, I decided to use this to my advantage.

"What kind of cigarettes are they?" I said as I approached her.
"They're Marlboro Lites."

"I prefer menthols," I said. "Do you mind if I have one?"

She opened the packet and held it out to me. I took one and she lit the end for me.

"I didn't know you smoked, Terry," she said with a surprised look on her face.

"Don't tell your dad," I said with a wink.

From then on, Barbara relaxed and began to open up. One day, she approached me with a question.

"Terry, I know you're from Liverpool. Did you grow up Catholic or Protestant?"

I thought this was an unusual question. She went on to tell me that two of her siblings had broken away from Judaism, one to become a Protestant and one to become a Catholic. She told me it had caused a problem in her family. I told her that same problem had been around for centuries in Britain and that I'd shrugged it off.

Davis began to open up to me also. Sometimes, I'd make him afternoon tea. I introduced him to Earl Grey with freshly- baked scones and jam. I told him that the Queen of England had afternoon tea regularly.

"I love the queen," he said.

I began to ask him questions. He had many unusual diplomas on his wall, and when I asked him what they were for, he told me he was a Master Mason and would often meet with the members of his lodge for lunch in Beverly Hills.

Once again, I became a companion and a therapist. He told me he regretted selling the company and that he missed his beloved, deceased wife, Rose. We were becoming close.

In the early mornings, I'd often take a walk around Arm and Hammer Park and think about my legal situation in England. The fact that I was still on the run was driving me crazy. My mind would oscillate between high anxiety and deep depression. I'd call my lawyer in England, Rob Brody, from the pay phone in the park, and ask him for advice. Most of the time, I would call him just to hear a friendly voice from home, and every time, he gave me the same, encouraging advice.

"Stay there and keep your head down, Terry," he'd say reassuringly. "Give it a little more time and then we'll see."

Sometimes, I'd meet with John Hammond, Richard Donner's butler. We'd drive to the park in our clients' Bentleys and chat like old friends, giving each other an insight into our clients' lives. On one occasion, John told me that Richard Donner was out of town and invited Annette and me to dinner.

When we arrived, John served us dinner and then gave us a tour of the house. He took us into a room that looked like an armory and showed us Donner's collection of guns. He told us about his interactions with Mel Gibson and Danny Glover and seemed to be enjoying his job. It was a fun night.

Barbara approached me a few days later and told me that her father's 75th birthday was coming up and wanted to know if I could organize a party for 12 family members. I told her I knew her father loved afternoon tea and asked her if she wanted me to set up a formal table with British fare. She was excited by the prospect.

I placed a pie and pastry order at the Tudor House, and on the day of the party, Annette and I collected a dozen of each pie and pastry from the bakery. We set the dining table up with the finest silver and crockery in the house, making sure it was thoroughly polished and tarnish-free. It hadn't been used since before his wife had died. We laid the food out, placing pies and pastries in alternating rows, with a large, English trifle placed symmetrically on both ends of the table. The party was a huge success. I'd never seen Davis nor Barbara so happy. The guests all made comments about the food, and by the time they had finished, not a morsel was left.

The guests began to leave as the evening wore on, and at the end, only Barbara and Davis were left. Annette and I cleaned up the dining room and kitchen. We were so busy, we didn't notice that Davis had entered the kitchen and was standing at the back with his nurse. He was wearing pajamas and a robe. I'd never seen him up this late before.

"Terry, this is for you," he said and he held a white envelope out towards me. He thanked me for his party and left.

I took the envelope and put it in a drawer for safe keeping. We were in the middle of cleaning the place and I didn't want to disturb the momentum by being distracted by its contents. When we finished our duties, I retrieved the envelope and opened it up. It contained 27 ten-dollar bills.

This was just the beginning of the fun I had with Davis. I had a friend at The Amfac Hotel in Los Angeles. The servers in the hotel restaurant were all budding actors and would perform a song and dance routine at regular intervals during Sunday brunch service. This friend invited me to brunch, so I decided to ask Davis if he'd like to come with Annette and me. He agreed.

We drove to the hotel in the Rolls Royce. There were four of us in the party: Annette, Davis, Maria (Davis' nurse), and me. The place was packed and full of life. My friend at the hotel told his colleagues that Davis, the Max Factor heir, would be arriving, and when we did arrive, they treated us like movie stars. We were seated in a booth and instantly served a complimentary bottle of champagne, with which we made mimosas. Davis chugged down his drink and then went to the buffet with Maria. He came back with a gigantic plate of food.

Maria looked worried. Davis was on a specific calorie-controlled diet, given to him by his physicians at Cedars Sinai Hospital. His weight was recorded daily, and if it wasn't maintained within a specific range, whoever was involved in the preparation and service of his food would be in danger of losing their job, when his daughter Barbara found out. I shrugged and smiled when I caught Maria's eye. She smiled back but I knew she was concerned.

A young, beautiful waitress made a beeline for Davis and sat on his knee. The crowd watched and listened as she sang the old

Judy Garland hit, "Somewhere Over the Rainbow." It was evident that Davis was loving it. He smiled and didn't take his eyes off her.

I started getting a little bit worried again when Davis went off to the buffet for the second time and came back with a massive plate of desserts. He chowed down on chocolate soufflé and apple pie and did so without a care. Maria and I locked eyes. I knew that this might just lead to trouble.

After the meal, I dropped Annette off at our apartment and then drove back to the house with Davis and Maria. Davis was tipsy. Maria and I each took an arm and walked him into the house. If Barbara had been there at the time, she would've gone berserk. Although it was early, Davis went to lie down on his bed. I asked Maria not to serve an evening meal and recommended a small snack and a glass of orange juice instead. She agreed.

The next morning, I arrived at work just in time for Maria to weigh Davis, as she did every morning. He weighed in at 201 lbs., which was 13 lbs. heavier than the 188 lbs. he had weighed the day before. I knew that Barbara would arrive soon and the first thing she would do was examine the records of Davis' heart rate, blood pressure and weight. I told Maria that if she wanted to keep her job, she should mark Davis' weight down as 189 lbs. With a little coaxing, she did just that.

Barbara arrived just a few minutes later, in her beautiful Jaguar XJ6. As soon as I heard her pull into the driveway, I walked out of the house to greet her.

"Good morning," I said. "Are you having a cigarette before you go in?" I asked.

"Yes, Terry," she said, and she handed me a cigarette out of the box.

She asked me how her father was after the brunch the day before. I told her that he'd enjoyed himself and that Maria and I had monitored his food intake to ensure he complied with his diet. She seemed happy. She told me that Davis was thrilled with his life now that I was around.

All good things must come to an end, but not every good

thing ends as abruptly as my job with Davis. My sister, Pat, was coming to see me for a vacation. I knew her plane would be landing at 5 pm. She would be staying with Annette in the apartment, so I planned on seeing her later in the evening. I was about to serve dinner one evening, when I got a phone call. I answered the phone in the kitchen.

"Are you Terry Moogan?" said the cold, emotionless, male voice.

"Yes,"

It was an agent with the Immigration and Naturalization Service.

"We have your sister here in custody and we've checked you out, Terry. You're not supposed to be in the country. We know where you are and we're coming to the house to get you."

I asked to speak to Pat, but the agent wouldn't let me. I slammed down the phone's receiver and sprinted to my living quarters. Davis and Barbara saw me running up the stairs and they followed.

"What's wrong, Terry?" said Barbara.

"I can't tell you right now, Mrs. Bentley, but I have to leave," I said as I hurriedly stuffed my clothes into bags.

Davis was mortified. As I ran out of the house, I could hear him shout, "We've lost Terry."

I drove frantically to the apartment in Santa Monica. Annette was shocked to see me. When I told her what had happened, she darted around the apartment, packing whatever clothes and possessions she could. I knew it was possible that Pat might get past immigration, so I asked a trusted neighbor to keep an eye out for her, just in case she arrived, and to have her meet us at a nearby Motel 6.

Later that evening, Pat met us at the motel and told us she had been apprehended on her way through the immigration check. The immigration agents had asked her to give them my information, and when she did, they made her wait a few hours and then released her. We were all shaken up over the ordeal. I called

Barbara Bentley to explain the situation, and when she asked me if I was coming back, I replied, "Not at this time."

After about two weeks, Annette and I returned to the apartment. I asked the neighbors if anyone had come to visit me during the time I was gone and I asked at the leasing office. I concluded that the INS agent who'd called me had lied just to scare me.

I'd enjoyed my time with Davis and decided to call around to the people I'd met during my tenure with him, just to maintain contact and explain the situation. One of those people was John Hammond, the butler to Richard Donner. His wife, Diane, answered the phone. I could tell by her tone that something was wrong. Diane informed me that John had committed suicide just a few weeks earlier, in Donner's house, using one of his firearms. Apparently, it had been a big news story but I'd been too wrapped up with work and I'd missed it. I was truly devastated. John was a good man and had been a good friend to me.

CHAPTER 33
SPIELBERG

I needed a job, so my next stop was The International Domestic Agency in Beverly Hills. Dora wasn't happy. As soon as I sat at her desk, she laid into me.

"What the hell happened, Terry? What the hell were you thinking?"

I just sat there and took her diatribe. When she finished, I waited a few seconds in silence, looking her straight in the eye.

"I'm an illegal alien," I said quietly. "The INS called the house and threatened to come and arrest me."

She shook her head and waved her hand in the air in a dismissive manner. She ignored my statement and quickly changed topics.

"I have two potential clients I think you'll be a perfect match for," she said calmly. "Steven Spielberg and George Segal."

I was obviously familiar with Spielberg, so I asked to be interviewed by him first. Dora picked up the receiver of the phone on her desk and dialed a number. She sat there staring at me until someone answered.

After a few minutes of small talk, she placed her hand over the mouthpiece of the receiver and said, "Can you be in Burbank on Wednesday at 11.30 am for an interview with Mr. Spielberg?"

I nodded in the affirmative.

That Wednesday, on the drive to Burbank from Santa Monica, in my red and white Cadillac Seville, I couldn't help but feel amazed at the fact that, here I was, a bank robber on the run from the police in England, on the way to interview for the trusted position as butler for the world's most famous film director. Spielberg was the brains behind such movie blockbusters as "Jaws" and "Close Encounters of the Third Kind," and had just seen the second installment of his Indiana Jones franchise become a massive hit.

I arrived at Warner Brothers studio just before 11.15 am. The guard at the gate took my identification and issued me a badge that had "Visitor for Mr. Spielberg" written on it. He then gave me directions to Spielberg's office and sent me on my way.

I drove past the various industrial-looking lots and stages until I finally arrived at a nondescript, chalet-looking structure on the side of the road. I exited the car, grabbed my briefcase, and brushed down my suit with my free hand before knocking on the door.

I'd thought that an assistant or intern would answer the door, but it was Spielberg himself. He was sporting his trademark mustache and glasses and wearing jeans and a woolen cardigan over a button-down shirt.

He invited me into his office. I'd been expecting something more opulent but it was quite plain. He motioned for me to sit in the chair in front of his desk as he sat opposite me. He seemed upbeat and excited about the meeting. He told me he had been interviewing potential house managers, but he preferred to have a butler. He then asked me about my life, my experiences, and my background.

When I finished my presentation, I knew from his affect that he wanted to hire me. He outlined his expectations. He told me he had two African Gray Parrots that he kept in the kitchen and they would be my priority in the house. He told me my most important duties would be to clean their cages, feed them, and groom them. What he said next actually shocked me. He told me the parrots were more important to him than his wife, Hollywood actress, Amy Irving. I made my mind up then and there that I didn't want to work for him.

The meeting lasted just over forty-five minutes. As soon as I got home, I called Dora and asked her to set up an interview for me with George Segal.

CHAPTER 34
GEORGE SEGAL

I arrived in Bel Air the following Monday and pulled the car up to the gates of a magnificent mansion, reminiscent of an English country estate, located on Sunset Boulevard. I pushed the button on the intercom and George Segal answered. He asked me to park the car in a space just inside the gate and told me he'd come out to meet me.

As soon as I got out of the car, I could see him briskly walking towards me, smiling, with his hand outstretched. Dora had told me that Segal was one of Hollywood's biggest stars and had co-starred in movies with the likes of Robert Redford, Rod Steiger, Barbara Streisand, and Glenda Jackson. Now, here he was, greeting me like we were old friends.

We walked together up the driveway to his house and he immediately began asking about me. He nodded as I told him about my experiences as a butler, and when I mentioned Elizabeth Taylor, he stopped me and said, "Don't be surprised if we invite her for dinner."

The house was as beautiful on the inside as it was on the outside. As we entered through the front door, we were greeted by a montage of black and white framed photos of all the stars he had associations with.

The living room was tasteful, spacious and opulent. The room was filled with beige and soft yellow leather furniture. He motioned for me to sit on a sofa and sat opposite me. He informed me that his wife would be arriving to meet me soon and then made small talk and built a rapport between us easily. He reminisced about his movie career and told me all about the movie "Who's Afraid of Virginia Woolf," that co-starred Elizabeth Taylor and Richard Burton and led to him receiving an Oscar nomination.

His wife, Linda, arrived moments later. She was beautiful, with long, black hair and her gray, fitted pantsuit gave her an executive quality. She was a manager in the music industry and her most famous clients were The Pointer Sisters.

She was just as friendly and as gracious as George. They took me on a tour of the house and finished up in the garage, where George introduced me to his red Aston Martin convertible and his white Rolls Royce, a Silver Shadow.

They led me out to their pool, which overlooked the Santa Monica Mountains, and as we sat on the poolside furniture, George asked me if I would serve at the poolside functions they hoped to organize. He then took me into his office and asked me if I would work for him. Of course, I said yes. I informed him that I'd discuss my salary with Dora, but if all went well in that regard, I'd be glad to take the job.

As soon as I arrived home, I called Dora and told her I wanted the job with George.

CHAPTER 35
LUNCH WITH THE A-LISTERS

I arrived early on a sunny, summer Monday morning and let myself in, using a code for the gate that George had given me. I opened my briefcase, grabbed a notebook and immediately got to work writing a syllabus for the upkeep of the house.

I was all alone for about an hour and then I heard George and Linda talking as they descended the stairs. They both seemed happy to see me. George marched toward me and shook my hand firmly.

"Great to see you, Terry," he said, before plonking himself down on a chair at the dining room table and grabbing a script from a pile right in front of him.

Linda busied herself preparing for the day. There were files, random papers, and personal items on the dining room table that she stuffed into her tote bag. She grabbed her briefcase, then tapped the pockets of her pantsuit, presumably making sure her keys were in the right place.

She kissed George on the forehead and said, "Have a good day, boys," before briskly walking out toward the garage, her high heels clicking on the marble floor.

George put down his script and pointed at the notebook I had in my hands.

"What've you got goin' on there?"

I sat down at the table and showed him my curriculum. I'd composed a list of duties and a timeline for their completion; cleaning, cooking, chandelier-polishing, and car maintenance. I informed him that I'd direct the gardeners and make him lunch at a time that would suit him. He nodded, smiled and grabbed his script again.

Later that day, I was in the garage, cleaning the Aston Martin. I got lost in my duties and hadn't noticed that George was standing right behind me. I pointed at a stack of framed posters piled up against the far wall and asked him if they were all posters of the movies he'd been in. He told me they were. I asked him if he wanted me to paint the garage and hang all the posters on the wall and he was thrilled.

"Really, Terry, you'd do that for me?" he said.

"Of course. It'd be my pleasure."

The next day, I painted the garage. As I was hanging the posters, I was amazed by the sheer number of movies George had starred in.

As the months drew on, we fell into a routine. I'd leave work at 5 o'clock, but I always prepared George and Linda's evening meal before I left. Most of the time, I'd make a stew and order a salad from Nate and Al's on Beverly Drive to complement it.

George liked me to drive him to lunch at The Brown Derby on Beverly Drive. I'd drop him off in the Rolls Royce and then spend an hour driving around and grabbing lunch for myself, while he dined with his friends, Hollywood legends like Buddy Hacket and Charles Durning.One day, he told me a friend who had arranged to have lunch with him had canceled at the last minute. He asked me to drive him to The Brown Derby in the Aston Martin. We drove out of Bel Air and south on Sunset Boulevard. We were both wearing white shirts and sunglasses and I couldn't help but feel the eyes of everyone around. I parked the car at the valet stand and he asked me to join him for lunch.

We dined and chatted like we were old mates. He told me about his friendships with Glenda Jackson and Elizabeth Taylor and asked me about my experiences growing up in Liverpool. I told him what I could. The irony of the situation wasn't lost on me. Here I was, a wanted bank robber from the streets of Liverpool, eating lunch in Beverly Hills with a Hollywood icon.

As the months drew on, George began to trust me more. I was puttering around in the kitchen one day, when he approached me with a request.

"I want to organize a garden party at the weekend. It'll be just me and a few guys. Can you help me out?"

Annette and I had nothing major in the works, nothing we couldn't put on hold, so I agreed.

"Of course I can," I said enthusiastically. "Do you want me to cook anything special?"

He slapped me on the shoulder. "We'll give 'em your good old Irish stew," he said. "Oh, and I'm going to need you to pick a few of them up."

Over the next few days, I began preparing. I collected the linen tablecloths and napkins from the cleaners, polished champagne flutes, 12-oz. beer glasses, and rocks glasses for the array of beverages I was sure they'd be partaking in. I also rubbed out the blemishes from the silverware.

On Friday evening, before leaving the house, I chopped carrots, new potatoes, and celery, and peeled boiled onions. I diced a slab of lamb loin and seared each piece before dropping it into a slow cooker containing seasoned stock I'd prepared earlier, and eight ounces of the best Cabernet Sauvignon, and then added the vegetables before closing the lid.

I arrived back early on Saturday morning and prepared the poolside patio. I covered the dining table with a freshly-ironed maroon cloth, created table fans from napkins for each setting, set out cutlery for three courses, and then prepped the outdoor bar with champagne buckets, polished glasses, Irish whiskey, and a polished, stainless-steel trough, filled with ice and a choice selection of American bottled beer.

As I was finishing up the minor details, George wandered out to the patio, wearing his pajamas and robe.

"Well done, Terry!" he exclaimed jubilantly. "This is just what I wanted. The whole place looks fantastic and that stew smells delicious."

I threw down the rag in my hand and began to walk toward the kitchen.

"Thank you, George. Let me get you some breakfast."

"Don't bother with that, Terry. I need you to pick up a couple of my guests. Use the Rolls Royce."

He handed me a piece of paper with two addresses on it and slapped me on the shoulder.

"Good work, Terry," he said and rushed back into the house.

I arrived in Holmby Hills and parked the car close to a large iron gate. I pressed the button on the intercom, and within a few seconds, I heard, "Hello?" from the speaker.

"I'm here to collect you, from Mr. Segal," I said.

"I'll be down in a few seconds," the voice answered.

I waited next to the car, and within a few short minutes, Burt Reynolds came bounding out of the gate. He was tall, slim, but at the same time, toned and muscular. He was wearing black cowboy boots, blue Levi jeans and a white shirt, tucked in with the top two buttons open. Burt was a major movie star. The films "Cannonball Run" and "Smokey and the Bandit" were box office hits.

He extended his hand. "What's your name?" he said with a large, playful grin.

"Terry," I said, as I opened the rear door for him.

"Pleased to meet you, Terry," he said.

He climbed into the back seat and I closed the door. As I drove away from his house, I wondered if I should start a conversation. Within a few seconds, he started one himself.

"Where are you from, Terry?" he said.

I answered him, looking in the rear-view mirror.

"I'm from Liverpool in England."

"That's where The Beatles come from, right?" he said.

I nodded in reply.

We made small talk, with the concentration on English music, and before we knew it, we'd arrived at a corner mansion on Roxbury Drive.

I left Burt in the car and walked through the open gate, up the drive, and rang the bell. A few minutes later, the door flew open and out came the comedian, Buddy Hackett. He was short and chubby. His hair was unkempt and salt-and-pepper in color.

He was wearing gray slacks, a patterned polo shirt, and a brown sports coat.

I'd heard of him, but didn't know much about him, other than the fact that he'd been in various movies during the sixties, but was best known as a stand-up comedian.

He introduced himself with a handshake and then patted his hip.

"I'm packing," he said, staring me in the face. "Are you packing?" he asked.

"I don't think so," I said.

I had no idea what he was talking about. He laughed and then walked off toward the car. I later found out that "packing" meant that he was carrying a gun. Burt and Buddy joked and laughed all the way back to the Segal house.

When we arrived, George was sitting on the patio with the actor George Durning, who looked to be in his mid-sixties. He'd starred in "The Sting" with Robert Redford, "Tootsie." with Dustin Hoffman, and had been nominated for the Academy Award for Best Supporting Actor for his roles in "The Best Little Whorehouse in Texas" and "To Be or Not to Be."

Burt and Buddy joined George and Charles at the table and I went to work. I asked if I could get them any drinks.

George pointed to a whiskey bottle perched on the bar and said, "That'll do, Terry, and no ice, it'll just dilute the whiskey."

Those around the table seemed to agree so I placed a shot glass in front of each of the guests and handed the bottle to George, who was waiting for it with his hand outstretched. He then offered his guests cigars.

I went back to the kitchen and began putting the finishing touches on the lunch when there was a knock at the door. When I opened it, Robert Redford was facing me.

"Come on in, sir," I said. "They're by the pool."

Redford nodded. "Thanks," he said and walked straight past me. He'd obviously been to the house before.

As I performed my duties, I could hear them talking. George seemed irritated. He slammed a script down on the table.

"I'm not doing it when Brando's getting fifteen million," he said.

Redford was taken by surprise. "Why are you bitching? It's not like you," he said.

I could tell that George was embarrassed by his outburst. He looked right at me and said, "Is that stew ready?"

I nodded, went back to the kitchen, and prepared bowls of stew and bread and then returned to the table and served them.

"Have you ever thought about being in the movies, Terry?" asked George in front of his guests.

"I am in the movies, sir," I said theatrically, "but you can't see me. I'm the butler, always in the background."

"There you go," said George, throwing his hands in the air. His guests laughed.

I returned to the kitchen and lost myself in my duties. I put the finishing touches on the berry trifle I'd made for their dessert and started to clean the kitchen, when George approached.

"They love the stew, Terry. Do you have any more?"

I nodded. As I was filling more bowls, I began to tell him about the time I'd spent with Laurence Olivier. I don't know why I said this, but I told him that, according to Olivier, Brando was the finest actor in Hollywood. I could tell that my words annoyed him.

"Just bring out the stew," he said and he returned to his guests.

As the afternoon drew on, I watched and listened to them from a distance. They were drinking and smoking and laughing. Their crude jokes and chest-puffing entertained me. They were really no different from the men of Liverpool I'd known throughout my youth.

About a week after the party, George asked me if I could stay into the evening to take care of a guest who would be arriving. I agreed. At just after six o'clock in the evening, there was a knock at the door and when I opened it, a tall, slim, fair-haired man smiled at me and told me that George was expecting him. He introduced himself as Harry, and when I told him my name, he remarked that I sounded like John Lennon.

He was singer-songwriter, Harry Nilsson. When the Beatles had been asked who their favorite American singer was, they'd unanimously chosen Harry. He told me of his friendship with John Lennon and Paul McCartney and seemed delighted to talk to an average stranger such as myself.

I escorted him into the garden, the place where George loved to entertain his guests. After feeding them, I was treated to a couple of hours of Harry singing, while George played the banjo.

I was getting ready for work one day, and when I turned the key in the ignition of my prized Cadillac, nothing happened. I frantically twisted the key again but the engine was dead. I called a tow truck, and while waiting for it to arrive, I called George to tell him that I didn't have transport to get to work. He asked me where I was getting the car towed to. I told him Mark C. Bloom on Wiltshire Boulevard.

I arrived at the mechanic's garage. It was a busy day. People crowded the waiting room and the front desk had a line of customers waiting anxiously to know the fate of their cars and bank balances after the work it would take to get them fixed.

After an hour or so, a mechanic in overalls approached me and told me the battery and alternator needed replacing. He then told me the car wouldn't be ready for at least a week. Just then, I heard a commotion outside. A car horn was being tapped and the people in the waiting room were running to the window and staring outside. George was outside in the Aston Martin. The top was down and he was waving for me.

"Come on, Terry," he shouted. "Let's go!"

I could feel everyone's eyes on me as I left the waiting room. I casually got into the passenger seat and George sped away. He loaned me that car until mine was back on the road. It dawned on me that George trusted me. He trusted me with his house, his belongings, and his life. The irony of being a wanted bank robber and being trusted by George, who was in the highest echelons of the Hollywood elite, wasn't lost on me.

The weeks went by. I loved working for George, but like all good things, it had to come to an end. He informed me one day that he was getting plastic surgery under the care of renowned surgeon Dr. Arnie Klein, who had worked on Michael Jackson and Joan Rivers. I'd met him once before at Mr. Weisman's house.

George gave me a list of vitamins and supplements to buy at Gelson's and then informed me that, after his recovery, he was moving full-time to New York to further his career. Needless to say, my job was done.

The following two weeks were tough for me mentally. As I cared for George during his post-surgery recovery, I tortured myself, going back and forth over the decision I was about to make. Now was the perfect time to face my demons. I'd have to discuss my next move with Annette, but I was almost certain of what that next move would be.

CHAPTER 36
FACING THE MUSIC

As I was driving home after my last shift for George, my mind was spinning. I parked the car, gingerly walked up the stairs and stood facing the apartment door for what seemed like hours but was only minutes.

I entered the apartment and Annette was waiting for me in the living room. She met me at the door as she oftentimes did and wrapped her arms around me. Her beautiful smile left her face when she sensed the anxiety in me.

"What's wrong, Terry?" she asked.

"I think it's time that I went back and faced the music," I said, searching her face for a clue as to how she would respond.

"Are you sure that's what you want, love?" she asked tenderly. "We've got a good life here. Do you really want to chance it?"

Life was good in Southern California. We both loved it but the shadow of prison had been looming over me for years, and even though we were living in paradise, the hell of my thoughts was too much to bear any longer. I sat on the couch and she sat with me, holding my hand in hers.

"I have to go back, love," I said. "It's the only way I can find peace."

We boarded the British Airways red-eye flight without any problems. It was 1986 and security wasn't as tight as it is today. I was nervous, but confident. I knew that Joey Wright had been found innocent, even though evidence had been "found" on him, so I thought my chances were good. Regardless of the outcome, I was still young and fit, and to top it off, I had my beautiful wife,

Annette, by my side. When I began to weigh things up, the pit of fear I had in my stomach began to dissipate and a warm sense of confidence replaced it.

We opened our passports as we reached the immigration desk and were just waved along. That was the first hurdle out of the way. We walked out of the arrivals lounge and into the cold air. It was April and had been warm and sunny in California when we left, but it was bloody freezing in northern England. The rain didn't help matters, either.

My brother, Alan, waved at us from across the street. He was leaning up against his car, wearing a parker jacket and gloves. I quickly put my arm around Annette and rushed her toward the car. Alan opened the rear door and Annette dove into the back seat. I got in the front.

"Do you want to stop for a pint before we go home?" asked Alan, who already knew the answer.

"Go on, then," I said. "I could do with a decent pint of Guinness."

We chatted and laughed and threw out all kinds of banter on the way back to Liverpool and acted like I'd never left. When we arrived in West Derby Village, we stopped at The Jolly Miller.

It was warm inside, and as I walked in through the doors, the familiar pub smells of stale beer and cigarette smoke brought back memories of simpler times. Annette and I sat at a table. Alan ordered two Guinness and a glass of white wine for Annette and brought them back to us. As soon as he sat down, we got to business.

"I called Rob Brodie a few times for an update on my case," I said. "Did you make an appointment for me?" I was hoping that Alan had done his due diligence.

"Yes," he answered. "You'll be meeting him in his office in the morning."

That was all I needed to know. Brodie had a reputation as a criminal's best bet at avoiding jail-time. If anyone could help me out, it was him. I could feel the jet lag setting in and Annette looked like she was about to pass out, so I asked Alan to take us home.

The next morning, we woke up to snow. It was bitterly cold, but the whole place was beautiful. I stared out of the window and captured the scene in my mind's eye. In just a few hours, I'd probably be handing myself in to the authorities at the direction of Brodie, so I wanted to enjoy the precious few moments of freedom I had left.

We arrived at Brodie's office at 9 o'clock in the morning. We were the only people there, the first problem of the day for the renowned criminal lawyer. Annette and Alan took a seat in the waiting room and Brodie's secretary led me into his office.

The mahogany wainscoting, bookcases filled with official-looking, ornately-bound legal books, and his large, almost regal desk, were reassuring. This was the office of a man who took his profession seriously.

Brodie waved me in as he looked up from the papers in front of him, while at the same time politely dismissing his secretary. He was a small, slim Jewish man, approximately 5 ft. 4in., with well-combed and greased black hair and round, gold-rimmed glasses. He looked like the last man you'd want at your side in a fist fight but his reputation as a trial lawyer proved that he was the first and only man you'd want representing you when you were standing in the dock.

"California's been good to you, Terry. You're looking well."

Without giving me the time to thank him for his observation, he immediately said, "Good news."

He turned the letter he was reading to face me and pushed it forward.

"I sent a letter to the Department of Public Prosecutions, asking to see if there were any active, outstanding warrants out for your arrest and they sent back this."

I looked down and couldn't believe my eyes when I saw the official letter. It was short and sweet. It read, "In regard to Terrence Moogan, there are no outstanding warrants for this man."

I would never have thought that a one-sentence letter could bring me so much relief and joy. I thanked Brodie, shook his hand and then walked out into the waiting room. Annette rose from her chair to greet me; I embraced her tightly.

We were all overjoyed. We walked through Liverpool City Centre and visited all my old stomping grounds. We drank a pint in every pub I'd frequented as a lad and I was greeted by all the old-time gangsters like a returning hero.

The prevailing question I kept getting asked was, "What are you going to do about Joey Wright?"

I knew Joey had worked with the police and informed on me in order to get a lighter sentence. He'd done a deal with the devil. He was an informer, a "grass" and that could not be tolerated.

My answer to that question was a resounding, "Maybe he's got it coming!"

CHAPTER 37
THE CONSPIRACY TO KILL JOEY WRIGHT

Two of my former partners in the Liverpool gangland were eager to see me. We had a history together. They didn't trust many men, but I knew they trusted me. For obvious reasons, their true names will remain anonymous, but to make things a little easier, I'll call them Jerry and John.

I met them in Jerry's house during the first week I got home. We were sitting in the living room having a can of beer and chatting about old times, when Joey Wright's name came up.

Jerry's mood changed instantly and he started to get angry.

"Joey grassed on you, didn't he, Terry?" he said.

"Yes, he did," I replied as calmly as I could.

"I've got a shotgun upstairs. I'll kill that fucker right now," he said, trying to control the tone of his voice.

He stood up, placed a cigarette in his mouth and lit it. His hands were shaking as he placed the flame of the lighter against the end of the cigarette.

John and I looked at each other, knowing that Jerry was deadly serious. He stormed out of the living room and up the stairs. He returned a few minutes later with a long case. He sat back down on the couch, opened the case, and pulled out a double-barreled shotgun. He snapped down the barrel and inserted two shells before violently snapping the barrel back into position.

"This is what he's gonna get," he said.

I knew he meant it. My heart was racing.

"Behave yourself," I said as calmly as I could.

He leaned forward. "I'm gonna go to his house on Queen's

Drive, and when he answers the door, I'm gonna blast his head off."

John was nodding and seemed excited about Jerry's proposal.

"That fucker grassed on us as well," said John. "He's making shitloads of cash from his little smuggling business. All the while, he's working with the police to take us down."

A thought crossed my mind.

"If he's got a smuggling business going, why don't we tax him? I'll go to his house, take him for a drink and tell him to give us £150,000. That'll be fifty grand each." I could see the two of them getting excited.

"I'll do it tomorrow," I said.

Their eyes lit up.

"All right," said Jerry. "I'm on board, but if he doesn't go for it, or tries any funny business, he'll get the business end of this shooter."

The next day, I got Alan to drive me to Queen's Drive. I asked him to wait for me, just out of sight of Joey's house. The house was a beautiful, detached dwelling that Joey had bought for cash with his ill-gotten gains. I casually walked through the garden gate, up the garden path, and knocked on the door. There was no answer, so I knocked louder. A few minutes later, a young, stocky man, with reddish hair and wearing an Adidas tracksuit, answered the door. He was one of Joey's sons. I'd known him as a child, but now he was a well-known gangster.

"What do you want?" he said in a gruff tone.

"I'm here to see Joey," I said.

He looked behind me and scowled. He wasn't used to people knocking on the door.

"Who are you?" he asked.

"I'm Terry Moogan," I said.

He smiled and shook my hand. His affect changed and he seemed pleased to see me.

"I'll go and get my dad," he said and shut the door.

A few minutes later, the door opened and Joey stepped out. He looked older and he'd put on weight since I'd last seen him. He looked surprised to see me and smiled nervously.

"Terry, it's great to see you. You look great," he said.

I didn't acknowledge his compliment "We need to talk, Joey. Can we go for a pint?" I asked.

"Yes, Terry," he replied. I could tell he knew there was something wrong.

"Come on, let's go to The Black Horse," I told him. He knew it wasn't a request. It was an order.

He grabbed a jacket from inside the door and nervously pulled it on. We walked together and chatted cordially. The small talk was mundane but Joey knew there was an underlying tension.

When we arrived at the pub, I ordered two pints of lager and directed him to sit at a table in the corner of the room. I sat with my back to the wall, facing the room and knew I had the upper hand. I took a sip of lager, gathered my thoughts and began.

"Joey, you've been talking to the police and Jerry and John are just as disappointed with you as I am. You can make it right, but it's gonna cost you £150,000."

He fidgeted in his chair. "I don't have that kind of money," he said.

"They're gonna hurt your family, Joey. It's in your best interest to pay up."

Joey looked down and shook his head.

"I know you were an informer for Detective Smith, Joey. Don't even try to deny it. If you don't pay up, the other two will destroy everything you hold dear and I'll be on a flight to Los Angeles."

"I'm sorry, Terry," he said. "How about £75,000?"

"The price is £150,000."

He looked at me and nodded.

I told him to be back at The Black Horse in three days at the same time with the money and I left him.

Three days later, I arrived back to the pub. I'd circled the place first and searched the car park for any sign of the cops, his associates or any type of an upcoming ambush. When I was satisfied that the coast was clear, I entered the pub.

I saw Joey sitting at the same table I'd left him at three days prior. He was wearing the same clothes, and due to the stubble he had on his face and the bags under his eyes, I would've thought he'd been there the entire time, if I wasn't aware of our business. I nodded at him and then scanned the pub for signs of his associates. There was no-one else around, apart from the barmaid and a couple of old men playing dominoes.

I sat down on the chair across from him. "Where's the money?" I asked.

Joey glanced down. Right there at his feet were two Tesco plastic carrier bags. He reached down to grab the bags and I stopped him.

"No," I said. "You're going to pick up those bags and carry them outside to a blue Ford Mondeo that's waiting in the far corner of the car park. Put the bags in the boot and walk away."

Joey nodded, and without saying a word, he picked up the bags and walked outside. I followed a short distance behind him and watched as he did just as I asked. Joey slammed the boot shut and walked away. We both knew we wouldn't be seeing each other again, not as friends anyway. When Joey was out of sight, Jerry walked over to the car and drove away.

By the time I got back to Jerry's place, the lads had already counted the cash and sorted it into three bundles of fifty grand each. They were delighted with the result and agreed with me that the plan was a far better choice than killing Joey.

That night, the three of us dined in the swanky Charlie Parker's Restaurant in Crosby. We drank champagne and chatted until the early hours. At the end of the night, I told them that Annette and I would be going back to California within the week. We had a new life chapter waiting for us. We felt we had the world at our feet and an additional fifty grand to get us started.

A few years after my trip to Liverpool, Joey Wright was followed on a train from Lime Street Station to Glasgow. From the train, he was followed to an apartment where he was arrested, along with three associates, by a joint task force from the Liverpool and Glasgow constabulary. Joey was found with four kilos of heroin and was immediately placed in custody, awaiting trial. All four men pled guilty before the trial, in the hope of a lighter sentence. The judge, however, made an example of them and sentenced each man to 21 years in prison.

While Joey was in prison, his son, Michael, who was the apple of his eye, was shot in the head and killed in his car at a drive-through KFC on East Lancashire Road.

Joey served eleven years in prison, during which time the authorities confiscated his house and cars. He became an alcoholic. One evening, after a binge-drinking session, Joey asphyxiated on his own vomit and died. That was the end of Joey Wright, the Reservoir Dog.

CHAPTER 38
CALIFORNIA DREAMING

Annette and I had left California with the prospect of me spending a few years in prison and thereafter spending the rest of our lives in England, but now we were back in Southern California, I had a clean record and we had £50,000 to start a new life.

We'd rented out our apartment in Santa Monica, so we got a hotel room until we got back on our feet. Annette and I came up with a plan. We'd market ourselves as a husband-and-wife domestic team. I'd be a butler and Annette would be a housekeeper and cook.

I called Dora at the International Domestic Agency in Beverly Hills, to see if she had any work for us.

"Terry, where have you been? I've called you so many times," she said with excitement.

I told her I had to take care of some personal business and that both Annette and I were looking for work together.

"I have just the job for both of you," she said. "Can you meet me at the office?"

Annette and I drove to Beverly Hills that day. Dora was waiting for us when we arrived. As we walked in through the door, Dora bounded off her chair and rushed to meet us, and then she got straight down to business.

"I have the perfect job for you both. Come and sit down," she said, as she led us to her desk. "I have a client in Orange County. He's an attorney. I called him to tell him about you as soon I heard you were back. He wants you to go for an interview."

"Orange County's a bit far," I said. "I don't know if I'd be interested."

"Terry, this is a live-in position. There's a house for you on his property. You're going to love this."

I turned towards Annette. She smiled and nodded.

"Ok," I said. "We'll go and have a look."

"Great," said Dora. "He wants you to go this Sunday at midday. Will that be alright?"

"Yes, that works for us," I said.

She pushed a manila envelope across the table. "This contains some information about the client and his estate. You should read it before the interview."

Annette and I read the dossier together. Terry Gee was a criminal attorney and was said to be one of the best in the United States. He came to fame representing the comedian, Richard Pryor, after Pryor poured flammable liquor over himself, set himself ablaze, and ran off down a busy Los Angeles Street during a drug-fueled episode in the 1970s. Gee represented him legally and then orchestrated a brilliant campaign to successfully rehabilitate the comedian's public image. A few years after the Pryor incident, Gee was contacted by a young, African-American staffer, who worked for The Reagan Administration, named Armstrong Williams, who asked Gee if he could convince Pryor to help the administration in the pursuit of making Martin Luther King Jr Day a federal holiday. The rest is history. Gee had also worked on some high-profile criminal cases, including the grisly Hillside Strangler case.

I'd had enough of attorneys through the years and wasn't sure if I wanted to work for one, but on that Sunday morning, Annette dressed in her gray jacket with matching skirt and a beautiful pink blouse, and I dressed in my blue suit, a pressed white shirt and red tie. We drove in my Mustang, south on the 405 freeway towards Orange County.

It took us just under an hour to get to Peacock Hill in the opulent surroundings of the Tustin Hills, and as we arrived, we were met with a set of massive, white wrought-iron gates and a 15 ft. high hedge.

We parked the car and exited. I pressed the button on the intercom. Within seconds, a voice from the speaker said, "Hello, this is Mrs. Gee."

"Hello Mrs. Gee," I responded. "This is Terry and Annette Moogan. We have an appointment with you."

"Come in. We'll be right there," she said, and the gate began to open.

As we walked through the gate, Terry and Patty Gee walked out of the house to greet us. Terry Gee was short, slim and well-groomed, with short, dark hair, parted at the side. He was wearing slacks and a blue sweater, similar to golfing attire. Patty was pale-skinned and dark-haired and radiated a natural, untouched beauty. She was dressed casually but her look exuded class.

They greeted us as if we were old friends, with handshakes and hugs, and immediately led us into the opulent 5,000 sq. ft. house. As we walked in through the front door, we were confronted by a gigantic chandelier over the spiral staircase. They took us into the living room, which was tastefully decorated with white shag carpets and beige leather couches. Gee asked us to sit down and offered us water. He told us what he was looking for and mentioned that a husband-and-wife team would be ideal for what he had in mind.

He asked me what type of meals we could cook.

"Everything from gourmet to home cooking," I said. "I'd start by composing a curriculum for the house."

"Let me give you a tour," said Gee.

He led us up a flight of stairs and out to the patio, with a full-sized swimming pool flanked by a Jacuzzi. We walked past the pool and into an exquisite cottage on the opposite side. It appeared to have been built and furnished as a type of cottage you'd find in the English countryside, rustic, with heavy wooden ceiling beans and leather-bound furniture.

"This'll be your home if you decide to work for me," said Gee.

He led us back to his primary residence and we walked up an external staircase, from which he pointed out the vast, green expanse, all five acres of which was his.

We walked in through the top floor. Before us was a thirty-five-seat cinema with a massive screen.

"This is where we watch movies with friends and family," he said. "You'll be welcome to join us."

We walked down an internal staircase and into their bedroom, where a king-sized bed was flanked by two his-and-hers walk-in closets. He took me into his closet, while Annette went with Patty into hers. Gee showed me his collection of bespoke suits and crocodile skin shoes.

"Would you mind shining these for me?" he said.

"Not at all. I'll add that to the curriculum," I responded.

We bypassed the ground floor, as that was where our initial meeting had taken place, and he took us straight down into the cellar, which doubled as a medieval-themed dining room and a climate-controlled wine cellar. The large, wooden table was surrounded by twelve leather-backed wooden chairs.

He opened a door in the dining room that led into a custom-built games room with a card table and a blackjack table.

"This is where we entertain," he said. "Don't worry, the kitchen's right above us and there's a dumb waiter over there that's connected to the kitchen."

Annette and I were impressed. I had already bonded with Terry Gee and Annette looked to be on great terms with Patty.

Gee took us to an external building, which comprised his office and a conference room. His office was modestly decorated and furnished, but the conference room was obviously built to send a message. A large, oblong table stood in the center of the room. The chairs surrounding it were maroon Chesterfields, imported directly from England. Leather maroon couches were scattered behind the chairs, giving the room a laid-back and casual feel, in contrast to the formal table.

Gee motioned with his hand for us to sit. Patty sat beside him.

"I feel really comfortable with you two," he said and smiled. "You're a beautiful, young couple. I like what I see. It would be a pleasure to have you here."

"Thank you, Mr. Gee," I said.

He nodded and looked directly at me. "What kind of car would you like if you moved here?" he asked.

I knew he was trying to buy us. I decided to play it cool.

"I already have a car, Mr. Gee," I answered. "I have to tell you that we're seriously thinking of going back to work for Davis Factor."

Gee leaned forward. "I'm gonna cancel the other interviews we've got scheduled for the position. How about I just give you some extra money every month?"

"Annette and I will discuss it over the week and let you know," I said, as I stood up and pushed the chair back into its original position.

Gee grabbed a notebook and pen off the table and scribbled down his number. He tore of the page and handed it to me.

"This is my personal number," he said. "Call me when you've made a decision."

CHAPTER 39
A NEW LIFE

Annette and I discussed the choice we had to make. On the one hand, we'd worked for Davis Factor before. The job was easy and we knew he loved us. On the other hand, the anxiety of the past was over, As I was no longer a wanted man. With this in mind, Annette and I unanimously decided to start a new life, and with a new life, comes new surroundings.

I called Terry Gee on the Tuesday after the interview and advised him that Annette and I could start work the following week and therefore asked if we could move in over the weekend. Mr. Gee was ecstatic.

We arrived on Saturday morning and were let in by one of the landscapers. We advised him that a moving truck would be arriving soon and made our way to our new home. As we walked through the front door, our attention was drawn to a table on which two beautiful bone china teacups and saucers were waiting for us. Between the cups was an envelope addressed to Annette and me. Annette opened the envelope and pulled out a card. The inscription in the card read, "Welcome aboard, from Patty and Terry."

The movers came and went, and during the evening, as Annette and I were putting the finishing touches on making the cottage our home, Mr. and Mrs. Gee came by. Annette made tea and we chatted like old friends. We agreed that Annette and I would use the rest of the weekend to settle in and that our days off would be Sunday and Monday. We would therefore begin work on Tuesday morning.

I asked Mr. Gee if Annette and I could walk the grounds to get a feel for the place. He graciously allowed us.

"Treat the estate like your own home, Terry," he said. "After all, it is your home now."

Annette and I walked through the pristinely-manicured estate. It was kept by a team of five full-time landscapers, who worked diligently to maintain the standards that Mr. Gee politely demanded. Every square inch of the place had a magnificent view of the mountains and the exquisite landscapes of Orange County.

After a walk of the grounds, we decided to view the garage. I knew Mr. Gee's taste demanded nothing but the best and I wasn't disappointed by his choice of cars. He had a dark blue Rolls Royce Phantom, a red Ferrari and a silver Mercedes SLC, all well-kept and newly washed.

Terry and Patty Gee seemed like wonderful people, but by the way they kept their estate, I could tell their standards were high and they would expect a lot from Annette and me. It was a challenge we both relished.

On the following Tuesday morning, I got to work on the curriculum. The house was massive and we'd been told to expect to cater for parties on the weekends, so we chose to use all day on Fridays to clean the house from top to bottom, in order to present a well-kept home for their guests.

Saturday mornings would be used to clean Mr. Gee's office, then make him and his wife lunch, which invariably consisted of a Sloppy Joe each. After lunch, Annette and I would set up for the parties in the evening.

The weekdays would be used for general maintenance, buying groceries, general cleaning and preparing the Gees' evening meals.

The following Saturday, Mr. Gee asked us to set up the main dining room for just him and Patty. I knew this would be a test to see just how well Annette and I could cook. We went through all our cookbooks and finally came a decision.

The dining room was as opulent as could be. It had gigantic windows that exposed the magnificent landscapes of Orange County. Its floor was made of the finest Italian marble. The central dining table was large enough to seat twelve people, and consisted of a two-inch thick glass tabletop, resting on three alabaster roman columns. The crockery was made of the finest, pure-white Staffordshire bone china, and the cutlery was 24-carat, gold-plated Sheffield steel.

We set the table up as I had done on the Queen Elizabeth II, with pink linen napkins, folded fan-wise, three sets of cutlery, and perfectly polished Waterford crystal wine glasses.

The meal consisted of veal piccata, served with strawberry sauce, on a bed of al-dente linguini and roast potatoes as a side. Dessert was our famous berry trifle, followed by Irish coffee.

Mr. and Mrs. Gee were thrilled. "If you keep cooking like this, you'll spoil our guests," said Mr. Gee with a smile.

We'd passed our first test. Mr. and Mrs. Gee were impressed.

The following week, Mr. Gee approached me. "Patty and I will be hosting a party on Saturday evening," he said. "We'll be inviting six guests."

I knew this would be another test. Now, Annette and I would have to impress a whole room of people.

By the time Saturday evening came around, Annette and I were ready. We both dressed in black suits, with white shirts and black ties. The only difference was that Annette wore a skirt and I wore well-pressed black slacks.

As the guests arrived, Mr. Gee introduced each of them to Annette and me. They met us as if we were old friends. Mr. and Mrs. Gee had told them all about us. They were building their ideal estate and it seemed that an English butler was a major part of it.

As they chatted among themselves, I served hors d'oeuvres of green olives wrapped in cream cheese and rolled in crushed walnuts cut in half on a silver tray lined with doilies.

When the guests formerly sat at the table, they were served sliced cranberry chicken breast in thousand island sauce on a bed of linguini that had been cooked with mint leaves. The meal was paired with Mr. Gee's favorite white wine, Pouilly Fuisse. Mr. Gee pointed out the array of colors, red, green and yellow. All the food was served by Annette and me on silver platters. We'd serve from the left and take each plate from the right.

When the meal had been served, Annette and I stood back and watched them thoroughly enjoy it. Whenever a plate was emptied, or a glass was drained, we'd approach with an offer of more. The evening was an overwhelming success. We'd passed our second test.

The following Monday, Annette and I were relaxing by the pool when Mr. Gee approached.

"Would you be interested in a tour of my car dealership?" he casually asked.

"Yes," we said in unison.

"Ok. Get ready. Meet me in the garage when you're ready. I'll drive," he said.

Mr. Gee owned the Toyota of Garden Grove dealership. Apparently, it was the third most lucrative Toyota dealership in the nation. When we arrived, Michael, the General Manager, was waiting for us. Mr. Gee told him who we were and he behaved like we were royalty. Michael took us around the whole dealership, explaining the intricacies of car sales and pointing out the various features of the new cars on the lot.

When we arrived in the showroom, there were two cars on display: a maroon Toyota Celica Sports GT and a black Toyota Supra.

"Which one would you like, Terry?" said Mr. Gee.

I was absolutely amazed. "The Supra," I said, without hesitation.

Mr. Gee instructed Michael to wash and prepare the car, and while he was doing so, Mr. Gee took Annette and me into his office, where I made tea.

We chatted for a while, and when Michael handed me the keys, Mr. Gee said, "Why don't you drive down the coast to Newport Beach and spend the evening by the beach?"

Annette and I said our goodbyes and then drove off in the new car. We exited the freeway on MacArthur Boulevard and turned south on Pacific Coast Highway, through Newport Beach and continued to Laguna Beach.

We parked at Heisler Park, high above the beach and nestled on the cliffs, and walked across the cliff tops, taking in the views of the aquamarine Pacific Ocean. We eventually arrived at The Cliff Restaurant and had dinner on the patio, high above the beach. We held each other and watched the sun go down until it disappeared over the horizon.

"We belong here," I said.

Annette just looked up at me and nodded.

The following week, a large van arrived at the house. Mr. and Mrs. Gee summoned us and said they had a special order that was arriving. The delivery driver drove through the gates and opened the back of the van.

"You're going to love them. They'll really add to your estate," he said.

Within a few short minutes, six peacocks majestically

trotted out of the rear of the truck. They were large and regal, with multi-colored plumes. Mr. and Mrs. Gee were thrilled. Over the following weeks, the peacocks would favor the gazebo for shelter and they were fed by the landscapers. They were a beautiful, welcome addition to the estate. The only problem Mr. Gee had with them was that they defecated all over the estate. I thanked heaven that the landscapers were responsible for dealing with that.

Annette and I would often lounge by the pool in the early evening, after our work day. On one of those evenings, Mr. Gee approached us.

"I'm having a special guest over for dinner on Saturday," he said. This was nothing new to us, so we took it with a grain of salt.

"Ok," I said. "We'll get a menu ready."

"It's Oprah Winfrey and her partner, Steadman."

"We'll sort it out for you, Mr. Gee," I replied.

Mr. Gee nodded. "She'll be here on Saturday at six. I want you to greet them at the gate when they arrive."

He turned on his heel and walked away. Annette waited for him to get out of sight.

"Did you hear what he said, Terry?" I could see she was both excited and nervous.

"Yes, I heard him," I said, without expression. I was used to meeting and serving the stars, so to me, it was just business as usual, but to Annette, this was a big deal.

"Terry, we're going to have to start planning for this now."

I groaned and slowly climbed up out of my lounge chair. "Ok, love," I said. "Let's get to work."

When Saturday arrived, we were ready. Annette and I waited at the gate. We arrived at precisely five-forty-five, so as not to keep our illustrious guests waiting. I was dressed in as close as I could get to Buckingham Palace livery, and Annette was dressed in her fitted black suit and tie.

Their limo arrived at exactly 5.45 pm. The driver exited the car and walked to the rear door. He opened the door and held out his hand. Oprah climbed out of the vehicle, clutching his hand, and then thanked him. Steadman got out of the other side and walked around to meet her. I introduced myself and Annette and they returned our greeting with a smile.

We walked them through the gate and past the house. Oprah commented on how beautiful the manicured lawns were and Steadman agreed.

As we got close to the gazebo, Mr. Gee saw them walking towards him. He got off his seat and jogged towards them. When he reached them, they all embraced. I could tell they were great friends.

"I see you met my butler, Terry, and his wife Annette."

"Yes," said Oprah. "I'm very impressed."

I asked Oprah and Steadman if they wanted a drink and they both ordered scotch with soda over ice.

They all sat together in the gazebo, surrounded by peacocks, with exquisite views of Orange County all around them.

After their welcome drinks at the gazebo, I approached the four and announced, "Dinner is served."

I walked in front of the group and led them to the main dining room.

Dinner was light and consisted of an appetizer of crab salad with hollandaise sauce, a main course of wild Alaskan steaks flambéed in brandy with a side of seasonal vegetables, and dessert was Battenberg cake a la mode, covered with milk chocolate flakes.

Annette and I were cleaning the kitchen as the guests were drinking coffee in the dining room. The door swung open and Oprah came in.

"I just wanted to thank you for the meal," she said.

We spoke for a while and she asked us where we were from. When we told her, she told us of her love for The Beatles, as people often do. She was gracious and seemed to really love her time with Mr. and Mrs. Gee

CHAPTER 40
THE TRIALS OF TERRY GEE

Terry Gee was a self-made man. He was one of the finest criminal attorneys in America, and as such, was always up for a challenge. The man was just always working. I admired him because, as one of the people Annette and I worked for, he was a special person.

As the months went on, we became close and he would confide in me about the events of his life and the decisions he had made as a result. I'd known many criminal lawyers – for obvious reasons! – and I knew that Mr. Gee had established one of the largest and most successful law firms in California and then had resigned from the firm to start a series of businesses that would eventually be known as Gee Enterprises. He then began to practice civil law, all the while keeping his successful business thriving.

"Why did you stop practicing criminal law?" I asked him one evening, while I walked the grounds with him.

"I just got disillusioned, Terry. I'd seen so many miscarriages of justice, but there was one case I was involved with that made me question everything I was doing."

I wasn't used to him opening up like this, so I just kept my mouth shut and listened.

"I got involved in a case a while back. An upholsterer from Garden Grove had been accused of attacking a woman and cutting her arms off. I defended him and he was found not guilty. A few years later, he was sentenced to death for the murders of two young women. As soon as I heard about the crime and his upcoming trial, I knew he was guilty."

I got the impression that Mr. Gee regretted defending him. He now practiced civil law only.

One of Mr. Gee's clients was Bill Maynard. Maynard had

founded Information Management Systems. IMS was responsible for creating the IMS AI 8080, which was one of the first personal computers on the market. Maynard went on to be the co-founder of the franchise ComputerLand, which by 1984, had reached over one billion dollars in revenue.

Maynard had been successfully sued by the company Micro Vest for 20 percent of the company and now Maynard wanted to sell the remainder of the company and cash out. Of course, Mr. Gee was chosen to be his attorney.

The legal proceedings were about to start, so Mr. Gee hosted Maynard at his home for three weeks prior to the proceedings.

"I need you to do me a favor," said Mr. Gee, while I was cooking his meal one Saturday evening. I looked at him and nodded. "I have a client who will be staying for a while and I'd like you and Annette to take care of him in the guest house."

"Of course, sir. It'll be our pleasure," I answered, as I invariably did.

The following Monday, Bill Maynard moved into our house and took over the self-contained upper floor. Mr. Gee's work had given him a keen eye and an in-depth knowledge of humanity. He was a great judge of character and seemed to understand the capabilities of those he met within seconds of meeting them. I'm sure things were no different with me. He took me aside the day Mr. Maynard arrived, and stared into my face.

"He's staying with me for protection," he said, "among other things. I'll need you to stay with him and take care of him."

I nodded. "Leave it to me, sir."

I could see him relax as I acknowledged his concern. I had the feeling that Mr. Maynard had enemies and I knew from experience that enemies and wealth were an equation that equaled extreme danger.

For the next three weeks, Mr. Gee and Mr. Maynard would work from Mr. Gee's office. During breaks, I'd take Mr. Maynard to Fashion Island, an exclusive shopping area. We'd have coffee and a chat and talk about life in general. He told me that his wife was in San Francisco at their house and he seemed excited at the prospect of seeing her again. We'd then go to Neiman Marcus, where he'd browse through the store. On a few occasions, he'd buy a designer suit and have one of the tailors make the necessary alterations.

When the day came for the real business to be negotiated, even I was nervous for the man. When they came back to the house in the evening, they were ecstatic. After Mr. Gee's legal wrangling, Bill Maynard was a couple of hundred million dollars better off.

For the next two days, Patty, Bill and Terry Gee partied at the house. In the mornings after breakfast, they'd sit out by the pool, and in the evenings, I'd drive Mr. Gee and Mr. Maynard in the Rolls Royce to Magic Island, a club that was owned by Mr. Gee.

Magic Island was unlike any other nightclub in Orange County. It was a gothic, theatre-style nightclub with a center stage adorned with gold-tassel trim, red velvet curtains, and circular tables, where magicians would roam and amuse the guests with sleight-of-hand and card tricks between stage performances.

Mr. Gee and Mr. Maynard would talk, laugh and drink for hours and I would sit at a table by myself and watch the room. On the second evening, their conversation turned serious. I tried to listen but the noise of the room drowned them out. I did, however, hear the word "taxes" being thrown around from time to time.

On the way home, Mr. Gee leaned over the headrest of my seat and gave me instructions.

"Bill's going to be leaving the house in the morning," he said. "Just prepare coffee at six. He won't have time for breakfast."

I nodded in reply.

The next morning was a whirlwind of movement. Mr. Gee arrived at the guest house at 6 am, exactly when Mr. Maynard and I were already flying around, packing his things.

I carried his bags to the gate, where a limousine was already waiting. Mr. Gee said his goodbyes, and as we turned to walk back to the house, Mr. Maynard called me back to the car.

"This is from me, Terry," he said, handing me an envelope. I took the envelope from him and immediately stuffed it in my jacket pocket.

"Thank you, sir," I said.

He looked me straight in the eye.

"Terry, you're the finest help I've ever had in my life."

He shook my hand, smiled, and disappeared into the car.

As we walked back, Mr. Gee told me that he and Patty would be leaving that day and going to meet the Maynards in Australia, where they'd be staying before escorting them to Hamilton Island.

"We need to pack, Terry. We'll be gone for two weeks. Just use the house as if it were your own."

Later that evening, I drove Mr. and Mrs. Gee to John Wayne Airport. When I got back, Annette was waiting in the house. I pulled out the envelope Mr. Maynard had given me and opened it. There was $10,000 inside!

"What's that for?" said Annette.

"It's just a token of appreciation from Mr. Maynard," I replied with a smile.

I learned later on that Mr. Maynard had fled the country due to a tax debt of over $100 million, spread out among numerous countries, including Singapore, Ireland and the United States. He remained in exile for years in Saipan, one of the Northern Mariana Islands, where he lived a low-key life. In 2011, he was found living on the Cayman Islands.

Annette and I lived in the main house for the next two weeks. I'd work out every morning; running, shadow-boxing and doing calisthenics, followed by a swim, and then the two of us would lounge by the pool for hours. In the evening, we'd eat dinner in the main dining room and then watch movies in the home cinema.

Two weeks later, I got a call at the house. It was Mr. Gee, informing me that they would be returning the following Monday. Annette and I got the house ready, just as they liked it, and when Monday came, I was waiting in the Rolls Royce, directly outside the airport's Arrivals gate.

As always, the Gees were happy to see me. I opened the rear passenger door and then closed it when they were comfortably seated. I then stacked their luggage in the trunk and took my place in the driver's seat. Mr. Gee instantly started a conversation.

"How's the house, Terry?"

"Everything's just as you like it, sir,"

"I don't know why I even asked that," he said. "Of course it is. Patty and I are lucky to have you."

He reached over the seat and patted me warmly on the shoulder.

Terry and Patty Gee were a fun couple. They were constantly entertaining guests and having parties. Christmas was a special time of year for them. No expense was spared on their lavish decorations and celebrations.

In the first week of December, Mr. and Mr. Gee summoned Annette and me to a meeting in Mr. Gee's office. When we arrived, they were sitting at the conference table and Mr. Gee was holding a manila file in his hand.

"We're doing something special this year," he said.

He motioned with his hand for us to sit, and when we did, he began to tell us his plans.

"This year, we've got a guest list of just over two hundred people for our annual Christmas party." He handed the file to me. "Their names and addresses are in the file. Instead of sending invitations, I'm going to have each one of them RSVP using a homing pigeon. I'll need you to deliver the pigeons. I'll give you two labels for each guest. One label has their name and a 'Yes' typed on it, the other has their name and a 'No' typed on it. They'll RSVP by attaching either one of the labels to the pigeon's foot and then letting it go." Mr. and Mrs. Gee were beaming over this idea. "What do you think, Terry?"

I knew this was going to be an absolute nightmare but I couldn't say that.

"It sounds like a fantastic idea, sir," I said, trying to sound enthusiastic. "When will the pigeons be arriving?"

"They should be arriving tomorrow morning," he said.

"Will they be flying back here?" I asked, hoping that the answer would be no.

"No. They'll be flying back to the owner of the pigeons and he'll mail the guest list to me when they're all back."

That was at least one small mercy. The next two weeks were as stressful as hell. The pigeons arrived on a special van in cages the next day. Annette and I collated all the names and addresses and cross-referenced them using a Thomas Guide in order to deliver the birds as efficiently as possible. I thought I'd be able to deliver at least thirty birds a day but I was wrong.

We'd call the houses of the guests each morning to inform them that we'd be delivering their bird that day, but we rarely got an answer. I'd arrive at each house, in the hope that someone was home. It was always hit and miss if the guest was there. More often than not, a housekeeper or a son or daughter of the guest would answer the door, someone who couldn't possibly answer the RSVP. Because of this, we'd have to return to the house at a later time or day.

Another problem we ran into was the reception the birds got. Most of the prospective guests were freaked out at the thought of handling a pigeon. I'd have to do the RSVP for them. It took me almost three weeks to finish the project, but it did get finished in time and the party went off without a hitch. On one of those days, I got pulled over by a cop for making an illegal U- turn, in an attempt to get to my destination faster. While speaking to the cop, I told him what I was doing and asked him if I could show him my live cargo. When I opened the back of the van, the cop laughed and let me go with a warning.

On Christmas Eve, Mr. and Mrs. Gee again summoned Annette and me to the office. We'd bought them a unique gift and this would be a good time to give it to them. I'd commissioned a helicopter to take an aerial photo of the estate. I then got the photo blown up and put on canvas. We arrived at the office and presented them with their gift. They were over-the-moon happy with it. Mr. Gee then handed me a card. Annette and I opened it together.

It read, "Christmas is the time of year to say we're glad you came into our lives; it was a happy day." Inside the card was a check for $10,000.

Just after Christmas, Annette and I came back to the house one Sunday evening to find that our place had been burglarized. The Gees had been out also, so after clearing our own house and making sure that no-one was still there, I locked Annette in safely and checked the main house, too.

When the police arrived, they told us that the house next door had similarly been burglarized. Some of our designer clothes and most of Annette's jewelry had been taken. When Mr. Gee arrived back, he wasn't happy. From that time on, he had armed estate security on the front gates and patrolling the grounds at intervals. His home contents insurance covered our loss for $35,000.

When he handed me the check he said, "There's a loaded thirty-eight under our bed, wrapped in a t-shirt. If anyone breaks in while you're here, you know where to find it."

Just before the summer of 1988, Mr. Gee asked me to help with his nightclub, Magic Island. He told me that the menu was dated and the staff didn't seem to be trained well. He asked if I could help him out by creating a menu and training the chefs and service staff. I was up for the challenge. It took me a couple of weeks, but by the time I'd finished, the employees seemed to have rekindled their passion for service. Mr. Gee was thrilled.

As a thank you, in June of that year, he sent my wife and me on an all-expenses paid trip to the Hyatt Regency Resort in Maui. For the next week, we were pampered in the Spa and lounged on Kā'anapali Beach in the daytime and then ate in the opulent Swan Court restaurant in the evening. It was a welcome respite.

A few months after our return, Annette informed me she was pregnant. I'd never been happier and I could tell that Annette was ready for motherhood. We organized a meeting with Mr. and Mrs. Gee as soon as I got the news.

Mr. and Mrs. Gee were waiting for us in the office when we arrived. They were their usual cheery selves and were eager for us to share with them what news we might have. But as soon as we told them, their mood changed. The smile dropped from Mr. Gee's face.

"I wish you would've told me you were going to have a family," he said, coldly. "I think you should move on."

I looked over at Annette and I could see the shock on her face.

"I could still work for you," I said. "I could be your house manager. We can adjust things to make everything move as smoothly as it does now."

Mrs. Gee turned away and her husband shook his head.

"I'm giving you one month's notice."

Over the next month, the atmosphere changed. Mr. and Mrs. Gee didn't treat us the same as before. They had become cold and distant. In the last week of our employment, Mr. Gee introduced me to the couple who'd be taking our place. They were a young Asian couple and seemed, on the surface, to be ideal for the position. But apparently they couldn't deal with the demands of the job and resigned within two weeks of being employed.

Annette and I had to make a plan. We had a child on the way and uncertainty lay ahead.

CHAPTER 41
THE BISHOP'S HOUSE 1989

After settling down in the Southern California city of Santa Ana, we welcomed the birth of our daughter, Kelly, who was born at Santa Ana Hospital. Our little girl was the most beautiful baby I had ever seen. My wife, Annette, and I named her after an actress we both greatly admired, Grace Kelly, who married Prince Rainier of Monaco.

However, the day we signed out at the hospital desk to bring Kelly home, we had a great shock. The hospital presented us with a bill for $15,000! I had nowhere near that kind of cash. Eventually, I ended up paying 7.5 on the dollar.

We had purchased a small quaint cottage on the border of Tustin and Santa Ana in Orange County and began our life as a real family. I had just started a window maintenance business with two partners, Bob and Michael. Our service included cleaning the windows of custom homes and my specialty was chandeliers.

Our first month in business, we made $9,500, aided by Annette who was our receptionist and booked the jobs. My Liverpool accent fascinated the American clients, and I was proud to work with them.

When Kelly was one month old, I received a phone call from the local office of the International Employment Agency.

"Terry?" a woman said. "Is this Terry?"

"Yes. How are you, Dora?"

"I have a part-time job for you with the Bishop of Orange County. You live there, correct?"

"Yes, ma'am."

I was immediately interested as I still owed plenty of money for the hospital bill.

"Can you set up an interview, please?" I asked Dora.

She told me that the position was for a chef at the Bishop's house on Glassell Street in the City of Orange. She arranged the interview for the following Monday afternoon, on April 2nd 1979 at 2 pm.

As usual, I dressed formally in my best suit and carried my letters of reference in a small case. Arriving ten minutes early at the surprisingly small Cape Cod-style house with green shutters and a blue front door, I rang the bell. I waited for a few seconds before the door was slowly opened by Bishop Norman McFarland himself.

"Hello, sir," I said, holding out my hand.

"I am pleased to meet you, Terry," he said, warmly welcoming me.

He led me into a dining room located in the center of the house, and we sat down. I noticed that the house décor was plain and bland, as was the old furniture, with everything smelling musty. The expression on the bishop's red face was jolly and his all-black attire was that of a priest. I noticed that his hair was silvery gray, parted at the side.

He began the interview by asking about my experience and asking if I could cook for six priests at night, from 4 pm to 9 pm. I said I could and told him about my menus. The Bishop appeared impressed by what I told him and added that he was also the Bishop of Los Angeles. I was offered the position. It consisted of cooking for the priests of Mater Dei high school, who would occasionally come for dinner when he conducted his meetings.

The first week of April was Easter. I cooked cranberry chicken and broccoli with cheddar cheese for them. The dessert was chocolate cake. Luckily, the diners seemed over the moon at the meal I produced for them.

The staff at the bishop's house included Maria, a cleaning girl from Mexico, who often said she wished she was home. Each week, I gave her a list of groceries to buy. By now, all the priests had expressed their pleasure and excitement at having me as their chef, especially the school principal, John Weiling.

One evening, I overheard them making fun of the cleaner, Maria, saying she did not clean well. I was asked to train her, which I did. I also trained another immigrant, a girl named Alene. She had shiny long black hair and deep brown eyes. My heart went out to her when I learned she was a single parent with two daughters. She thanked me for my concern.

After I let myself into the house a week or so later, I heard noises upstairs. A woman in a nurse's uniform came down the staircase and introduced herself to me.

"I am Frances," she said.

"Nice to meet you. I'm Terry."

She explained that there was a patient upstairs and I asked if he would be needing dinner that night. Suddenly, the front door opened and Bishop McFarland appeared.

"Hi, Terry, I hope all is well," he said. Then, to my amazement, he rushed madly up the stairs. Within 15 minutes, he had come back down to the kitchen where I was cooking.

"Terry, we have a situation here," he said. "We have a patient. Would you like to come up and meet him? I've told him all about you."

I felt obligated to do as the bishop asked, and made my way upstairs to a bedroom he indicated. It held a double bed and a side table holding several containers of pills and medicine.

My eyes went instantly to the figure in the bed. I knew his name. He was Father Jack Lord. He was lying there with his eyes sunken, I could see, almost to the back of his head. An IV drip was connected to his left arm. As I stood looking down at him, he focused his gaze and stared at me. He looked ill, just skin and bones.

"This is Terry," McFarland explained to Father Jack. "He is a fine man."

"Nice to meet you," I said.

"Hi, Terry," he responded faintly, barely able to speak, his breath shallow.

I could see he was so weak he was unable to raise his hand to shake mine. He tried to have a conversation with me as to where I was from, as most people do when they hear my Liverpool accent, but it was hopeless. Nurse Frances just stood there and smiled at me. Then she turned to him.

"No talking, Father Jack," she said, cutting short his attempt to speak. "You must rest now."

I was wondering what was wrong with him, with a million possibilities rushing through my mind. He looked to be on his deathbed. Why wasn't he in the hospital? He reminded me of my childhood as the memories of the abuse from the Christian Brothers came flooding back.

Then it dawned on me that there was an AIDS epidemic just beginning. I figured out that this priest must have contracted the deadly disease. But I said nothing. I kept it under my hat and became a silent observer.

A few days later, I visited him with a special treat of English roast potatoes that I had parboiled, then roasted in oil. He managed to eat half of one potato, and thanked me. Then he said that perhaps tomorrow he could come down to the dining room, as all the other priests were going to be away at a baseball game at Mater Dei high school. It was obvious Father Jack didn't want to be seen, and I wondered if the other priests even knew he was upstairs, except for Bishop McFarland.

The following evening, I arrived at the house at 6 pm, carrying a bag of Kentucky Fried Chicken that Jack Lord had requested. I made my way upstairs to his room. He lay in bed, looking gaunter than ever.

"Hello, Father," I said. "How are you?"

He indicated he was too weak to move.

"Would you like me to carry you downstairs? I can do that if you like," I said.

He seemed amazed at my offer and attempted a smile. Then, with a great effort, he pulled back the bed covers, although how he managed to do so, I have no idea. Then Nurse Frances came bustling in, having heard my suggestion. She seemed nervous.

"It's okay," I told her.

Then I turned to the priest and told him to put both of his arms around my neck. I had to help him but I knew that his weight would be slight when I lifted him up. I remember thinking it was lucky I was pretty strong, although I could feel his brittle bones digging into my muscles.

"Hold tight!" I said as I began the walk down the staircase with him.

"You are a good man, Terry," he whispered in my ear.

When we reached the dining room and I placed him on a chair at the large table, he seemed confused, perhaps because no one else was there, but he managed to thank me. I told him I had his favorite KFC chicken, and a chocolate milkshake. The nurse had followed us down from his room and tried to interfere, but I assured her I had control of everything. Father Jack was too weak to eat on his own, so I went to work cutting up the chicken into small pieces and feeding them to him.

He took three mouthfuls and a few sips of the milkshake before I could see he was trying to tell me something. I understood that he wanted to go back upstairs. I suppose the effort had been a little too much for him but I was glad I had brought him down. I told him to put his arms around my neck as before, and I returned him to his room.

"God bless you," he whispered, the words almost too faint to hear.

I placed him gently back on the bed and pulled up the covers. As he lay there, with no emotion on his face, he stared at me as if committing my face to memory. I just smiled back and wished him goodnight.

I continued to carry on my duties for the other clergy, cooking and serving them their meals, but my attitude had changed. At home, I explained the situation to Annette, telling her that I was becoming really disgusted with the way the priests talked and joked about things at the table, their language coarse and vulgar.

"We will have some boys over at the weekend, at my place,"

one of them had remarked with a smirk. The others smiled and nodded.

It was obvious to me that they were homosexuals. I didn't care about their sexual orientation but I did object to pedophiles. I decided to leave the job and take my departure within a few weeks.

The following Monday morning, I arrived early to help Maria clean the house. There was silence from upstairs. I usually heard Nurse Frances walking around. I told Maria I'd go up and say hello to Father Jack. When I reached his room, it was empty and the bed had been stripped bare. I learned that he had died the weekend before of AIDS. That afternoon, the phone was ringing off the hook. I answered the first call.

"Hello, this is the Los Angeles Times," said a voice at the other end of the line. As soon as I heard those words, I told the caller he had the wrong number, and I hung up.

A few hours later, Bishop McFarland arrived, looking extremely agitated. I said nothing. That evening, there was a somber atmosphere in the dining room, with most of the priests eating their meal in silence. After dinner, I informed Bishop McFarland that I would be moving on and had decided to make my exit the following week to focus more on my business. However, I only lasted another two days. I couldn't take it any longer. Being around these horribly abusive priests gave me the creeps.

"Please send my check," I told the bishop, "to my home address in Santa Ana."

"Thank you, Terry," he said, with a worried look on his face.

I found out later in the news that Bishop McFarland had been hiding Father Jack Lord in a 'secret place' due to the situation and that the Catholic priest had died of AIDS and was a child abuser. That 'secret place' was, of course, the bishop's home, the diocese on Glassell Street, where I had been employed.

There was a settlement of $3.4 million for sex abuse against Father Lord. According to a confidential police file, it was revealed there was also a $100 million settlement for other clergy abuse.

McFarland was cited too, for helping to shelter priests for additionally-admitted molestations. In one instance, files and depositions showed that the bishop allowed a 15-year-old girl to stay at the diocese.

I tried for many years to put the Father Jack Lord experience behind me, but accusations against Catholic priests have continued to dominate the news occasionally, even to this day.

CHAPTER 42
THE MAN IN THE MOON 1996

After leaving the bishop's employment I carried on with our window maintenance business, which we would expand to north, south, and central Orange County. I offered a service to clean chandeliers. I had learned this skill on the Queen Elizabeth II ship, as well as in Beverly Hills.

In Newport Beach, California, there were exclusive mansions on Lido Island and along the coast. One particular area was called Harbor Ridge, where the homes were built on a hill overlooking the beach.

I received a call from a young lady, Mary Slemmons, at one of these homes, to give her an estimate to clean the chandelier. I arrived there close to 11 am. The guard at the security gate knew I was coming. I gave my name and entered the compound. I went to the street she had given me, Cherbourg. All the street names were in French. Her house was a custom mansion, overlooking Newport Beach. I rang the bell.

I was greeted by a lady who opened the door.

"Hello, I am Mary Slemmons," she said.

"Hi, I am Terry Moogan."

"This is the chandelier I'd like cleaned."

She pointed to a lighting fixture that was quite a bit smaller than I was used to cleaning. I gave her a price of $250 and said I could come the following day to do the job.

The next morning, I entered her home with my ladders, took every piece off the chandelier and cleaned it carefully by hand, using a mixture of hot water and vinegar. Then I put the entire chandelier back together.

Afterwards, Mary and I had a chat. She told me her husband,

Jim, owned the Newport Mercedes dealership. I told her I had a dinner menu for eight people to offer hosts who entertained in Newport Beach. I told her I did the cooking with my wife, Annette.

"I'll get you the menu, it's in my truck," I said.

Mary read the menu through and looked as if she was over the moon to have this kind of butler service. She selected veal piccata with raspberry sauce. I told her the dessert on the menu was always English trifle.

"Are you available Saturday?" she said.

"Yes, with pleasure."

"Good. We are set for Saturday."

To my surprise, she said that one of the couples being invited were Mr. and Ms. Buzz Aldrin. He was the famous astronaut who was the second man to walk on the moon and performed three space walks as a pilot on the 1966 Gemini 12 mission, as well as the 16 Apollo II mission. I knew the first man to walk on the moon was Neil Armstrong, the mission commander. I told Mary I was tremendously excited to be meeting the internationally famous astronaut.

Annette and I did the shopping necessary for the Saturday dinner, and arrived at the Slemmons' home at 5 pm. We set the dining room table and added pink and white rose bouquets at each end. We prepared the dinner. I was still in a state of excitement, anticipating meeting the man who had walked on the moon.

At 6 pm, the doorbell rang and I ran to answer it. The guests had arrived. It was Buzz Aldrin.

"Good evening," I said. "My name is Terry."

"Hi, my name's Buzz and this is my wife, Lois."

"Nice to meet you," she said.

I escorted them to the balcony and asked the Aldrins if they would like a drink.

"Yes, gin and tonic."

He seemed to be a friendly man, with grey hair and a red face. His wife was petite, with blonde hair.

After I served the drinks, I returned to the kitchen to help Annette. Then another four guests arrived and they joined everyone on the balcony. It was a lovely summer evening. The meal was ready, and the guests and hosts sat down at the dining table.

We served a spinach salad with strawberries, and poured white wine, a Pouilly Fuisse. During the deep conversations they were having, I served the veal piccata, while Annette poured the wine. Buzz looked up at me.

"Are you from the UK, Terry?"

"Yes, sir,"

"Beautiful meal," he said.

All the other guests joined in with appreciative comments about the dinner, which we finished with the trifle and strawberries. At the end of the evening, while the guests went to the patio, Annette and I cleaned up the kitchen and dining room.

While we were thanking the Slemmons prior to leaving, Lois and Buzz Aldrin came into the kitchen.

"Terry, can I speak to you?"

"Of course, sir."

"The dinner was wonderful. We are having a party in a few weeks at our home in Laguna Beach. Could you and Annette come there to serve the same meal?"

"Of course. We would be delighted."

"Great. Let me give you my phone number," said Buzz Aldrin. "We will see you soon."

Within a few weeks, I got the call from Lois, who left a message on our phone asking us to call back. We did so and scheduled the Aldrins' dinner for a Saturday in late August.

We made our way to their address, a red brick house, overlooking the ocean. It was a beautiful summer evening.

Buzz answered the doorbell and invited us in. We were ushered through a marble-floored lobby with a chandelier in the center, and into the kitchen. It had a fabulous Wolf stove, which I knew cost thousands of dollars and was wonderful to cook on. The dining room was off the kitchen, and six large chairs upholstered in white velvet were placed around the table. We set the plates and silverware up and Annette placed a vase with white roses in the middle.

"Hello, Terry," said Lois when she came into the kitchen, talking as if she had known us for years.

The guests arrived at 6 pm. They were the Slemmons and a Mr. and Mrs. Gray. I served them appetizers on the patio where they sat around a log fire, and Annette poured the wine. Buzz came into the kitchen.

"It's great to have you. Are you a butler, Terry? You are amazing."

I had a question I'd been longing to ask.

"Have you ever flown in a G-4 plane Lear jet?"

"Yes," he replied, as I knew he would.

"The Apollo 11 would have been faster, right?" I said.

He laughed.

He went back to the dining room and I served the salad course, then the veal piccata. Mr. and Mrs. Slemmons were delighted. Then they all went outside to the log fire again, where I took them dessert and coffee. When I went to their guest bathroom at the side of the house next to an office, I took a peek inside. The walls were covered with photos of Neil Armstrong and Buzz Aldrin on the moon. It was an amazing sight.

After Annette and I cleaned up, I asked the Aldrins if everything was all right before my wife and I left. It was 9.30 pm. They hugged us and said that if they needed us again, they would call. As for us, we were still thrilled we had cooked dinner for the Man on the Moon.

CHAPTER 43
JAIL IN THE USA - THE $3 MILLION HEIST

Two men were arrested in 1979 for a $3 million heist on the docks in Liverpool. They were held without bail at the Risley Remand Centre in Liverpool, where I was awaiting my own trial. One of the men was Gerry Connor, the brother of world boxing champion, John Connor. I knew of his name but I had never met him. I encountered him on a staircase landing in the prison. I said hello. The other man, Peter, was from the City Centre. On the exercise yard a day later, I struck up a conversation with Gerry and Peter, and the three of us would eventually become good friends.

News of Gerry Connor being arrested for the $3 million robbery spread like wildfire through the prison, but when the three of us got together, we didn't discuss our cases. That was something that prisoners just didn't do.

I was found Not Guilty and released. Their trial would take place a month after mine. Peter always told me the police had no evidence and he, too, was found Not Guilty. Gerry, however, was not so fortunate and was sentenced to five years in prison. When Peter was released, I drove down to pick him up and took him and his wife home to celebrate.

A couple of weeks later, Peter confessed to me he had some of the stolen traveler's checks from the heist. He needed to raise £5,000 and asked me to meet him at the City Centre pub, the Beehive, the following day. I agreed. We met at the back of the pub, where we felt it would be safe and private.

"Do you want a deal, Terry? I will give you $25,000 in traveler's checks, in exchange for £5,000."

I took the deal, and years later, I decided I would go to Disneyland in Anaheim, California and use up what remained of my checks. I went alone. I was completely confident that the Happiest Place on Earth would accept my checks, even though one vendor became suspicious, but I ignored her.

Suddenly, I was surrounded by six policemen and taken to the Security Building, then transported to the Anaheim police station. I was charged with three felonies. I hired John Barnett, a famous California attorney, to defend me. At a cost of $7,500, which I agreed to pay, he informed me that I could be imprisoned for three to five years.

"What shall I do?" I asked. "Leave the country or stay?"

Since by that time, Annette and I had a daughter who was an American citizen, I made up my mind to stay. After a month of going to court, John Barnett struck a deal with the prosecutor at the District Attorney's office in Santa Ana. I was to spend 18 months in prison and pay restitution of $25,000. I took the deal. In 1993, the judge sentenced me to 18 months. My wife, Annette, was in the courtroom, crying.

I just smiled as the judge commented, "See you, son."

I was brought down to the cells and waited with the other prisoners, who were mostly from Mexico. They called me The Englishman Gangster. Then we got onto a bus and were taken to the Orange County jail, where we were finger-printed, then allocated a 'tank,' a dorm that accommodated 50 prisoners. The noise was horrendous with all the Mexicans yelling, and a smell of urine. I soon learned that I would be transferred to the James Music Open Prison, a farm, instead of staying at the top-security prison I was now in. I couldn't wait to leave.

I was assigned to a top bunk and another prisoner slept down below. At approximately 5.30 am, loud Vietnamese music was played to wake us up each day. I looked around. I felt as if I was in a nuthouse. I grabbed my clothes and jumped down to the floor from my bunk. The guy below stared angrily at me.

"Get your mother-fucking boots off my bed," he screamed. "Or I will fuck you up!"

I had made the mistake of placing my boots at the end of

his bed, in order to lace them up. I knew then that I would have trouble with him. One prisoner told me the man considered himself King of the Dorm. I decided that, with my fighting skills, I could take care of him. I had ordered some cigarettes, even though I didn't smoke, and some other items, such as biscuits and toothpaste. Every morning, we were allowed half an hour for smoking before we went to breakfast.

My plan was to wrap a towel around my fist and hide it behind my back. When he put the cigarette I offered him into his mouth, I would aim a blow at his jaw. It worked perfectly. He fell like a ton of bricks, banging his head on the wall. One of the prisoners, a black guy from the Bahamas, was as shocked as everyone else when he saw what happened.

"Pick him up," I said, "and tell the guard he fainted."

My bunkmate was taken to the hospital for observation. When he returned a week later, he was assigned to a different bed, and never said a word to me. I carried on my duties as a cleaner in the hut, as they called it. By now, I had become a superstar to the prisoners! I gave the Mexicans boxing lessons in the mornings, and then the blacks at night. It felt good to be so well respected. Annette visited once a week, while our daughter, Kelly, was told that her father was away, working on a boat.

I did my time and was released nine months later. During the process, I was asked if I had a Green Card that would allow me to stay and work in America. I responded that I would be going back home to England. My partners were taking care of the business and had remained loyal to me.

I did, in fact, carry on with my life and with my business. But it was always in the back of my mind to obtain a Green Card. Would the lack of one catch up with me one day?

CHAPTER 44
DEPORTATION TRIAL

The knock on the door early in the morning was unusual at 6 am. I thought I was in the middle of a dream. It was approximately nine months after my release from prison. I jumped out of bed and went to the front door. There were four FBI agents, who identified themselves to me. They were all wearing dark suits and I found the entire situation rather odd. But in a flash, I knew what they were going to say before they uttered the words.

"Mr. Moogan, you are under arrest! We have a warrant."

I got some clothes on.

"Put your hands behind your back."

They snapped the cuffs on me. I said goodbye to Annette. "I'll be back soon," I told her.

I was escorted to a black Crown Victoria Town Car and seated in the back. When we drove away, I noticed another car following us. It had black-tinted windows.

The man in the passenger seat next to the driver turned to me.

"Mr. Moogan, you are going to the detention center," he said. "You will have a hearing with an immigration judge."

We arrived at the center in Santa Ana. It resembled a prison. However, the agents were polite and explained my rights to me. When I was placed in a cell with a steel-rimmed toilet, my mind flashed back to when I was a child, and then to all the cells I had been in throughout my life. I asked if I could make a call home. My request was granted. I called Annette and told her the situation. She was, naturally, both concerned and angry.

"I told you to get your U.S. citizenship," she shouted into the phone. "But you were a know-it-all and wasted time while I went ahead and got mine."

"How is Kelly?" I said.

"She's fine."

"I'm going to court this afternoon, Annette."

"Do you want me to come?"

"No. Take care of Kelly. I will see you later."

I was given a lunch of spam and a cookie, and a small carton of milk. I ate and drank it all, even though I didn't want to. The guard began a conversation with me.

"Where are you from, Terry?"

"The U.K., Liverpool. What do you think will happen to me?"

"I'm not sure," he said, then answered my question about what time the court was in session by telling me that I would be in court within an hour. It surprised me that it would be so quick.

Finally, my cell door opened and I was told to follow the guard to the court and into a caged dock. The judge sat in his chair, surrounded by assistants.

"Do you have an attorney, Mr. Moogan?" he asked.

"No, sir."

"Do you understand why you are here? Under the U.S. immigration law and the Constitution, you broke the law. You committed three felonies in 1992, and served several years. Is that correct?"

"Yes, sir."

"This qualifies you automatically for deportation, to be deported to the original country from which you came. You will have to appear in court in Los Angeles, on Olive Street, to meet with an immigration judge. Do you own your own home, Mr. Moogan?"

"Yes, sir."

"Do you have a family?"

"Yes, sir."

"Where do you work?"

"I have my own business."

"That's good. I am going to release you, and a court date will be scheduled for three weeks hence, downtown. Do you understand?"

"Yes, sir.

"If you don't show up, you will be arrested. Wait for the paperwork to take with you today and you will be released immediately."

After 20 minutes, I received the documents, went outside the courthouse, and hailed a taxi. I was home 15 minutes later. Annette and Kelly greeted me at the door and we all hugged. I told my wife I was anxious to get back to work but she told me I had an interview the next morning with an immigration attorney she already knew, John Alcorn.

The next day, we arrived at Alcorn's elegant office lobby in Irvine, Orange County, California. The walls were covered in diplomas. One highly impressed me; a photo of him with the pope. Alcorn popped his head out of his office and invited my wife and me inside. His office was stunningly furnished with a red sofa and chairs and a beautiful desk. He offered a firm handshake.

"Why didn't you come to see me last year," he said, "when Annette advised you to?"

"Sorry, that was a bad mistake," I said.

"Do you want citizenship now?"

"Yes."

"Tell me about your life, Terry," he said, appearing to take a liking to me.

I told Alcorn most of it but kept back several incidents. He expressed great surprise at some of my exploits and vowed to protect me and my family.

"What is your fee?" I said.

"$15,000."

My heart sank at the amount.

"I will pay you $10, 000," I said.

"Agreed. Would you like some coffee or some English tea?"

"Yes, thank you. Tea sounds great. So, what do you think, John?"

"Terry, we have a good chance of winning."

"My felonies were dropped to misdemeanors."

"Really? That makes your case stronger, plus you wife is a

citizen, as is your daughter. Come back in three weeks. I will drive you to court for your appearance."

I did as he proposed and he drove us north along the 405 freeway, which was jammed with traffic as usual. During our trip, he told me he had never lost a case. I was beginning to feel more and more confident.

The courthouse on Olive Street was chaotic and pandemonium reigned. John took us up to the third floor, where we stood outside a courtroom. I was the only white guy in the crowd waiting to enter. The others were of all nationalities but mostly South American. When our case was called, we went inside and John approached the judge and told him I wished to have a trial. The judge agreed and set the date for July 29, 1994, at 2 pm, which was just two months away.

After we left the courthouse, John told me to come to his office the next day with a list of all the good deeds I had performed while in America. I told him about my work with the Catholic Church for five years as a volunteer.

"That's great, Terry. Please get a reference from them."

"I'll go and see Father Conlon. I also worked for the Bishop of Orange County, John McFarland, and I took care of a priest who was dying of AIDS."

"We'll use that information, too, at trial," John said.

Back at his law offices, he told me he'd see me soon. I got into my car and drove home. Over the next few weeks, I carried on my life and my business. During this time, I visited Father Conlan and informed him of my situation.

"I am a good man but we all make mistakes," I reminded him. "As a man of the cloth, would you give me a reference?"

He thought about my request for a few moments, and finally agreed, saying, "Alright, but Terry, don't ever get in trouble again."

"I won't, Father."

The next reference was from John Wilsing, the principal of Mater Dei high school, who also agreed to provide me with a reference. So, now I believed I had my 'tools' all ready. I met John Alcorn a week before the trial date and we finalized our plan.

"I want to defend myself by testifying," I said. "I have done public speaking as a Toastmaster."

John expressed great surprise, probably due to my Liverpool accent, which was nowhere near the posh accents heard in London and other places.

"Yes," I continued, "I have been awarded a high degree from that organization and I was president and Toastmaster of the Year."

"All right, Terry. Let's go get 'em."

The court date arrived. The night before, I thought up a special plan. I would take seven friends to court as my witnesses to give evidence of my good character. I had studied the law and I was primed and ready.

We all entered the courtroom: Annette, John, me and the Magnificent Seven! The prosecutor, a young man in a black suit, read the charge. John told the judge that Mr. Moogan wanted to be cross-examined by the People. The prosecutor told the judge that I had committed three felonies and that I should be deported.

"All right," said the judge. "Thank you." He turned to me. "Mr. Moogan?"

"Your Honor, I have paid for my crimes. I have done more good than bad in my life, sir. My wife and daughter are U.S. citizens. The scales of justice are uneven and do not appear to be in balance for me to be deported. I would like to share a story for the court, Your Honor. I was hired by the Bishop of Orange County to be the chef for the priests from Mater Dei high school in Santa Ana. I also took care of a priest dying of AIDS and fed him with a spoon, during which time I had no worries for myself, despite the disease the man had. I have given my services to the Catholic Church for five years and helped disabled people."

Everyone in the court, including the judge, was silent and appeared riveted by my testimony.

"I also served as a Toastmaster for 16 years," I continued, "and was president of the Irvine Toastmasters. I taught immigrants English. I have brought seven witnesses to court today, Your

Honor, to provide their testimony as to my character, that I am a good person."

I waited for the judge's response. Instead, he asked the prosecutor if he had any more questions.

"Yes, Your Honor, I do." The prosecutor turned to me. "Do you, Mr. Moogan, read books?"

I paused for a moment before saying. "Yes, I do. I particularly enjoyed 'The Power of Now,' by Eric Toll. I also read the books of Dr. Norman Vincent Peel. Of all the books I have read in my life, his books became my Bible."

We waited with bated breath for the judge's next words.

"I cannot break a family up," he said. "Mr. Moogan's felonies were dropped to misdemeanors. I hereby give my decision. Mr. Moogan, please stand."

I stood up as straight as I could, dreading to hear the fatal words the judge might utter.

"Mr. Moogan, you will not be deported. You are not to commit any further crimes. Your Green Card will be re-instated. Thank you. This case is closed."

I let out the breath I had been holding.

We all left the courthouse a happy family, big grins on our faces. John Alcorn congratulated me and we all went off for dinner. The attorney became my best friend. But our friendship was not to last long. I was devastated when he was killed in a car accident, taking his two-year-old child trick-or-treating on Hallowe'en.

CHAPTER 45
GOD MUST HAVE KEPT ME ALIVE FOR A REASON: REDEMPTION

The probability of being deported and separated from my family was a massive wake-up call. I had, in fact, already made up my mind to turn my life around and the judge's decision to allow me to remain in America was the final thump on the head that I needed.

Redemption is a big word. For me, its meaning has the great strength and inspiration that, in 1994, provided me with a 180-degree shift in my attitude towards my life of crime. It meant, personally, that I could take control of my life. I wanted to be a husband and father with no feelings of guilt. I thought about some of the people I had stolen from, such as bank customers, and others who through no fault of their own became victims because of me. Of these, too, I wanted to relieve myself of guilt and feel remorse.

Then I thought of some of the good things I had managed to do, such as caring for and feeding the priest dying of AIDS, and my five years as a volunteer and usher with the Catholic Church, despite the abuse I suffered at their hands. When I opened the safe at Mr. Weisman's home, I realized I could not steal his $155,000 in cash and jewels. When I handed them over to his security guards, I experienced a surge of good feelings. No guilty conscience this time! It was the right thing to do.

I also thought about the good I did for my employees when I was a butler and managed to improve their lives. I thought of the young drug addict I helped, and the immigrants I taught English. I reminded myself of the Toastmasters I served for 16 years, and my agreement not to call the cops at the desperate urging of Chet Hanks, Tom Hanks' son, when he begged me not to report a car accident, despite the neck surgery I needed as a result of his driving.

I remembered the many homeless people on the street I helped out, and my sympathy without judgement for the down-and-out men and women with mental health problems, and others who needed my help in paying the rent, although I knew it was killing them to ask me for a favor. I also thought of the woman whose life I saved when she tried to commit suicide by inhaling toxic fumes through a hose in her car.

With all this good that I was able to do by stepping up to the plate, the best of all was to marry Annette and have a wonderful daughter, Kelly. My heart overflows with love when I think how they stuck by me. I remember thinking, too, of the miracle when I was released from custody early due to the prison strike, and how God brought all those Hollywood stars into my life when I was their English butler, and the celebrities I met while in their service. I think of all the lawyers who believed in me when I didn't believe in myself, and how they successfully steered me through the rough spots.

After all the trials and tribulations I endured as a child and an adult, I am convinced that the Lord gave me the strength to tell the story you are reading. If I could start again, I would take the advice of Elizabeth Taylor to go into the movie business and become an actor. Who knows, I may still do so!

I am filled with hope, thanks to my belief in redemption. Hope is a good thing and good things never die.

MY SPIRIT

You can't kill my spirit
You tried many times
Even before Thatcher
And all of her crimes
I carried injustice
On my shoulders of steel
I still hold a smile
After the hurt I feel
I still sing with laughter
My heart's full of song
The courts shunned me
When I did nothing wrong
I fought till the end
My feet solid on the ground
In the web of abuse
Stronger spirit can't be found

If you have enjoyed this book, we appreciate your Amazon reviews and check out Terry Moogan's podcast interviews on Shaun Attwood's YouTube channel: From Liverpool Bank Robber To Hollywood Butler

OTHER BOOKS BY GADFLY PRESS

By Charlie Seiga:
Killer
The Hyenas
Liverpool's Notorious Jelly Gang

By John G Sutton:
HMP Manchester Prison Officer: I Survived Terrorists, Murderers, Rapists and Freemason Officer Attacks in Strangeways and Wormwood Scrubs

By Lee Marvin Hitchman:
How I Survived Shootings, Stabbings, Prison, Crack Addiction, Manchester Gangs and Dog Attacks

By William Rodríguez Abadía:
Son of the Cali Cartel: The Narcos Who Wiped Out Pablo Escobar and the Medellín Cartel

By Chet Sandhu:
Self-Made, Dues Paid: An Asian Kid Who Became an International Drug-Smuggling Gangster

By Kaz B:
Confessions of a Dominatrix: My Secret BDSM Life

By Peter McAleese:

Killing Escobar and Soldier Stories

By Joe Egan:

Big Joe Egan: The Toughest White Man on the Planet

By Anthony Valentine:

Britain's No. 1 Art Forger Max Brandrett: The Life of a Cheeky Faker

By Johnnyboy Steele:

Scotland's Johnnyboy: The Bird That Never Flew

By Ian 'Blink' MacDonald:

Scotland's Wildest Bank Robber: Guns, Bombs and Mayhem in Glasgow's Gangland

By Michael Sheridan:

The Murder of Sophie: How I Hunted and Haunted the West Cork Killer

By Steve Wraith:

The Krays' Final Years: My Time with London's Most Iconic Gangsters

By Natalie Welsh:

Escape from Venezuela's Deadliest Prison

"**A cross between** *Shawshank Redemption* **and** *Escape from Alcatraz!*" – **Shaun Attwood, YouTuber and Author**

All his life, 'Johnnyboy' Steele has been running. Firstly, from an abusive father, then from the rigours of an approved school and a young offenders jail, and, finally, from the harshness of adult prison. This book details how the Steele brothers staged the most daring breakout that Glasgow's Barlinnie prison had ever seen and recounts what happened when their younger brother, Joseph, was falsely accused of the greatest mass murder in Scottish legal history.

If Johnnyboy had wings, he would have flown to help his family, but he would have to wait for freedom to use his expertise to publicise young Joe's miscarriage of justice.

This is a compelling, often shocking and uncompromisingly honest account of how the human spirit can survive against almost crushing odds. It is a story of family love, friendship and, ultimately, a desire for justice.

By Ian 'Blink' MacDonald:

Scotland's Wildest Bank Robber:
Guns, Bombs and Mayhem in Glasgow's Gangland

As a young man in Glasgow's underworld, Ian 'Blink' MacDonald earned a reputation for fighting and stabbing his enemies. After refusing to work for Arthur "The Godfather" Thompson, he attempted to steal £6 million in a high-risk armed bank robbery. While serving 16 years, Blink met the torture-gang boss Eddie Richardson, the serial killer Archie Hall, notorious lifer Charles Bronson and members of the Krays.

After his release, his drug-fuelled violent lifestyle created conflict with the police and rival gangsters. Rearrested several times, he was the target of a gruesome assassination attempt. During filming for Danny Dyer's Deadliest Men, a bomb was discovered under Blink's car and the terrified camera crew members fled from Scotland.

In *Scotland's Wildest Bank Robber*, Blink provides an eye-opening account of how he survived gangland warfare, prisons, stabbings and bombs.

By Michael Sheridan:

The Murder of Sophie:
How I Hunted and Haunted the West Cork Killer

Just before Christmas, 1996, a beautiful French woman – the wife of a movie mogul – was brutally murdered outside of her holiday home in a remote region of West Cork, Ireland. The crime was reported by a local journalist, Ian Bailey, who was at the forefront of the case until he became the prime murder suspect. Arrested twice, he was released without charge.

This was the start of a saga lasting decades with twists and turns and a battle for justice in two countries, which culminated in the 2019 conviction of Bailey – in his absence – by the French Criminal court in Paris. But it was up to the Irish courts to decide whether he would be extradited to serve a 25-year prison sentence.

With the unrivalled co-operation of major investigation sources and the backing of the victim's family, the author unravels the shocking facts of a unique murder case.

By Steve Wraith:

The Krays' Final Years:
My Time with London's Most Iconic Gangsters

Britain's most notorious twins – Ron and Reg Kray – ascended the underworld to become the most feared and legendary gangsters in London. Their escalating mayhem culminated in murder, for which they received life sentences in 1969.

While incarcerated, they received letters from a schoolboy from Tyneside, Steve Wraith, who was mesmerised by their story. Eventually, Steve visited them in prison and a friendship formed. The Twins hired Steve as an unofficial advisor, which brought him into contact with other members of their crime family. At Ron's funeral, Steve was Charlie Kray's right-hand man.

Steve documents Ron's time in Broadmoor – a high-security

psychiatric hospital – where he was battling insanity and heavily medicated. Steve details visiting Reg, who served almost 30 years in a variety of prisons, where the gangster was treated with the utmost respect by the staff and the inmates.

By Natalie Welsh:

Escape from Venezuela's Deadliest Prison

After getting arrested at a Venezuelan airport with a suitcase of cocaine, Natalie was clueless about the danger she was facing. Sentenced to 10 years, she arrived at a prison with armed men on the roof, whom she mistakenly believed were the guards, only to find out they were homicidal gang members. Immediately, she was plunged into a world of unimaginable horror and escalating violence, where murder, rape and all-out gang warfare were carried out with the complicity of corrupt guards. Male prisoners often entered the women's housing area, bringing gunfire with them and leaving corpses behind. After 4.5 years, Natalie risked everything to escape and flee through Colombia, with the help of a guard who had fallen deeply in love with her.

By Shaun Attwood:

Pablo Escobar: Beyond Narcos

War on Drugs Series Book 1

The mind-blowing true story of Pablo Escobar and the Medellín Cartel, beyond their portrayal on Netflix.

Colombian drug lord Pablo Escobar was a devoted family man and a psychopathic killer; a terrible enemy, yet a wonderful friend. While donating millions to the poor, he bombed and tortured his enemies – some had their eyeballs removed with hot spoons. Through ruthless cunning and America's insatiable appetite for cocaine, he became a multi-billionaire, who lived in a $100-million house with its own zoo.

Pablo Escobar: Beyond Narcos demolishes the standard good versus evil telling of his story. The authorities were not hunting Pablo down to stop his cocaine business. They were taking it over.

American Made: Who Killed Barry Seal? Pablo Escobar or George HW Bush

War on Drugs Series Book 2

Set in a world where crime and government coexist, *American Made* is the jaw-dropping true story of CIA pilot Barry Seal that the Hollywood movie starring Tom Cruise is afraid to tell.

Barry Seal flew cocaine and weapons worth billions of dollars into and out of America in the 1980s. After he became a government informant, Pablo Escobar's Medellin Cartel offered a million for him alive and half a million dead. But his real trouble began after he threatened to expose the dirty dealings of George HW Bush.

American Made rips the roof off Bush and Clinton's complicity in cocaine trafficking in Mena, Arkansas.

"A conspiracy of the grandest magnitude." Congressman Bill Alexander on the Mena affair.

The Cali Cartel: Beyond Narcos

War on Drugs Series Book 3

An electrifying account of the Cali Cartel, beyond its portrayal on Netflix.

From the ashes of Pablo Escobar's empire rose an even bigger and more malevolent cartel. A new breed of sophisticated mobsters became the kings of cocaine. Their leader was Gilberto Rodríguez Orejuela – known as the Chess Player, due to his foresight and calculated cunning.

Gilberto and his terrifying brother, Miguel, ran a multi-billion-dollar drug empire like a corporation. They employed a politically astute brand of thuggery and spent $10 million to put a president in power. Although the godfathers from Cali preferred bribery over violence, their many loyal torturers and hitmen were never idle.

Clinton, Bush and CIA Conspiracies: From the Boys on the Tracks to Jeffrey Epstein

War on Drugs Series Book 4

In the 1980s, George HW Bush imported cocaine to finance an illegal war in Nicaragua. Governor Bill Clinton's Arkansas state police provided security for the drug drops. For assisting the CIA, the Clinton Crime Family was awarded the White House. The #clintonbodycount continues to this day, with the deceased including Jeffrey Epstein.

This book features harrowing true stories that reveal the insanity of the drug war. A mother receives the worst news about her son. A journalist gets a tip that endangers his life. An unemployed man becomes California's biggest crack dealer. A DEA agent in Mexico is sacrificed for going after the big players.

The lives of Linda Ives, Gary Webb, Freeway Rick Ross and Kiki Camarena are shattered by brutal experiences. Not all of them will survive.

Pablo Escobar's Story (4-book series)

"Finally, the definitive book about Escobar, original and up-to-date." – UNILAD

"The most comprehensive account ever written." – True Geordie

Pablo Escobar was a mama's boy, who cherished his family and sang in the shower, yet he bombed a passenger plane and formed a death squad that used genital electrocution.

Most Escobar biographies only provide a few pieces of the puzzle, but this action-packed 1000-page book reveals everything about the king of cocaine.

Mostly translated from Spanish, Part 1 contains stories untold in the English-speaking world, including:

The tragic death of his youngest brother, Fernando.

The fate of his pregnant mistress.

The shocking details of his affair with a TV celebrity.

The presidential candidate who encouraged him to eliminate their rivals.

The Mafia Philosopher

"A fast-paced true-crime memoir with all of the action of Goodfellas." – UNILAD

"Sopranos v Sons of Anarchy with an Alaskan-snow backdrop." – True Geordie Podcast

Breaking bones, burying bodies and planting bombs became second nature to Two Tonys, while working for the Bonanno

Crime Family, whose exploits inspired The Godfather.

After a dispute with an outlaw motorcycle club, Two Tonys left a trail of corpses from Arizona to Alaska. On the run, he was pursued by bikers and a neo-Nazi gang, blood-thirsty for revenge, while a homicide detective launched a nationwide manhunt.

As the mist from his smoking gun fades, readers are left with an unexpected portrait of a stoic philosopher with a wealth of charm, a glorious turn of phrase and a fanatical devotion to his daughter.

Party Time

An action-packed roller-coaster account of a life spiralling out of control, featuring wild women, gangsters and a mountain of drugs.

Shaun Attwood arrived in Phoenix, Arizona, a penniless business graduate from a small industrial town in England. Within a decade, he became a stock-market millionaire. But he was leading a double life.

After taking his first ecstasy pill at a rave in Manchester as a shy student, Shaun became intoxicated by the party lifestyle that would change his fortune. Years later, in the Arizona desert, he became submerged in a criminal underworld, throwing parties for thousands of ravers and running an ecstasy ring in competition with the Mafia mass murderer, Sammy 'The Bull' Gravano.

As greed and excess tore through his life, Shaun had eye-watering encounters with Mafia hitmen and crystal-meth addicts, enjoyed extravagant debauchery with superstar DJs and glitter girls, and ingested enough drugs to kill a herd of elephants. This is his story.

Hard Time

"Makes the Shawshank Redemption look like a holiday camp."
– NOTW

After a SWAT team smashed down stock-market millionaire Shaun Attwood's door, he found himself inside Arizona's deadliest jail and locked into a brutal struggle for survival.

Shaun's hope of living the American Dream turned into a nightmare of violence and chaos, when he had a run-in with Sammy "the Bull" Gravano, an Italian Mafia mass murderer.

In jail, Shaun was forced to endure cockroaches crawling in his ears at night, dead rats in the food and the sound of skulls getting cracked against toilets. He meticulously documented the conditions and smuggled out his message.

Join Shaun on a harrowing voyage into the darkest recesses of human existence.

Hard Time provides a revealing glimpse into the tragedy, brutality, dark comedy and eccentricity of prison life.

Featured worldwide on Nat Geo Channel's Locked-Up/Banged-Up Abroad Raving Arizona.

Prison Time

Sentenced to 9½ years in Arizona's state prison for distributing ecstasy, Shaun finds himself living among gang members, sexual predators and drug-crazed psychopaths. After being attacked by a Californian biker, in for stabbing a girlfriend, Shaun writes about the prisoners who befriend, protect and inspire him. They include T-Bone, a massive African American ex-Marine, who risks his life saving vulnerable inmates from rape, and Two Tonys, an old-school Mafia murderer, who left the corpses of his rivals from Arizona to Alaska. They teach Shaun how to turn incarceration to his advantage, and to learn from his mistakes.

Shaun is no stranger to love and lust in the heterosexual world, but the tables are turned on him inside. Sexual advances come at him from all directions, some cleverly disguised, others more sinister – making Shaun question his sexual identity.

Resigned to living alongside violent, mentally ill and drug-addicted inmates, Shaun immerses himself in psychology and philosophy, to try to make sense of his past behaviour, and begins applying what he learns, as he adapts to prison life. Encouraged by Two Tonys to explore fiction as well, Shaun reads over 1000 books which, with support from a brilliant psychotherapist, Dr Owen, speed along his personal development. As his ability to deflect daily threats improves, Shaun begins to look forward to his release with optimism and a new love waiting for him. Yet the words of Aristotle from one of Shaun's books will prove prophetic: "We cannot learn without pain."

Un-Making a Murderer:
The Framing of Steven Avery and Brendan Dassey

Innocent people do go to jail. Sometimes mistakes are made. But even more terrifying is when the authorities conspire to frame them. That's what happened to Steven Avery and Brendan Dassey, who were convicted of murder and are serving life sentences.

Un-Making a Murderer is an explosive book, which uncovers the illegal, devious and covert tactics used by Wisconsin officials, including:

– Concealing Other Suspects

– Paying Expert Witnesses to Lie

– Planting Evidence

– Jury Tampering

The art of framing innocent people has been in practice for centuries and will continue until the perpetrators are held accountable.

Turning conventional assumptions and beliefs in the justice system upside down, *Un-Making a Murderer* takes you on that journey.

HARD TIME BY SHAUN ATTWOOD
CHAPTER 1

Sleep deprived and scanning for danger, I enter a dark cell on the second floor of the maximum-security Madison Street jail in Phoenix, Arizona, where guards and gang members are murdering prisoners. Behind me, the metal door slams heavily. Light slants into the cell through oblong gaps in the door, illuminating a prisoner cocooned in a white sheet, snoring lightly on the top bunk about two thirds of the way up the back wall. Relieved there is no immediate threat, I place my mattress on the grimy floor. Desperate to rest, I notice movement on the cement-block walls. *Am I hallucinating?* I blink several times. The walls appear to ripple. Stepping closer, I see the walls are alive with insects. I flinch. So many are swarming, I wonder if they're a colony of ants on the move. To get a better look, I put my eyes right up to them. They are mostly the size of almonds and have antennae. American cockroaches. I've seen them in the holding cells downstairs in smaller numbers, but nothing like this. A chill spread over my body. I back away.

Something alive falls from the ceiling and bounces off the base of my neck. I jump. With my night vision improving, I spot cockroaches weaving in and out of the base of the fluorescent strip light. Every so often one drops onto the concrete and resumes crawling. Examining the bottom bunk, I realise why my cellmate is sleeping at a higher elevation: cockroaches are pouring from gaps in the decrepit wall at the level of my bunk. The area is thick with them. Placing my mattress on the bottom bunk scatters them. I walk towards the toilet, crunching a few under my shower sandals. I urinate and grab the toilet roll. A cockroach darts from the centre of the roll onto my hand, tickling my fingers. My arm jerks as if it has a mind of its own, losing the cockroach and the toilet roll. Using a towel, I wipe the bulk of them off the bottom bunk, stopping only to shake the odd one off my hand. I unroll my mattress. They begin to regroup and inhabit my mattress. My adrenaline is pumping so much, I lose my fatigue.

Nauseated, I sit on a tiny metal stool bolted to the wall. *How will I sleep? How's my cellmate sleeping through the infestation and my arrival?* Copying his technique, I cocoon myself in a sheet and lie down, crushing more cockroaches. The only way they can access me now is through the breathing hole I've left in the sheet by the lower half of my face. Inhaling their strange musty odour, I close my eyes. I can't sleep. I feel them crawling on the sheet around my feet. *Am I imagining things?* Frightened of them infiltrating my breathing hole, I keep opening my eyes. Cramps cause me to rotate onto my other side. Facing the wall, I'm repulsed by so many of them just inches away. I return to my original side.

The sheet traps the heat of the Sonoran Desert to my body, soaking me in sweat. Sweat tickles my body, tricking my mind into thinking the cockroaches are infiltrating and crawling on me. The trapped heat aggravates my bleeding skin infections and bedsores. I want to scratch myself, but I know better. The outer layers of my skin have turned soggy from sweating constantly in this concrete oven. Squirming on the bunk fails to stop the relentless itchiness of my skin. Eventually, I scratch myself. Clumps of moist skin detach under my nails. Every now and then I become so uncomfortable, I must open my cocoon to waft the heat out, which allows the cockroaches in. It takes hours to drift to sleep. I only manage a few hours. I awake stuck to the soaked sheet, disgusted by the cockroach carcasses compressed against the mattress.

The cockroaches plague my new home until dawn appears at the dots in the metal grid over a begrimed strip of four-inch-thick bullet-proof glass at the top of the back wall – the cell's only source of outdoor light. They disappear into the cracks in the walls, like vampire mist retreating from sunlight. But not all of them. There were so many on the night shift that even their vastly reduced number is too many to dispose of. And they act like they know it. They roam around my feet with attitude, as if to make it clear that I'm trespassing on their turf.

My next set of challenges will arise not from the insect world, but from my neighbours. I'm the new arrival, subject to scrutiny about my charges just like when I'd run into the Aryan Brotherhood prison gang on my first day at the medium-security Towers jail a year ago. I wish my cellmate would wake up, brief me on the mood of the locals and introduce me to the head of the white gang. No such luck. Chow is announced over a speaker system in a crackly robotic voice, but he doesn't stir.

I emerge into the day room for breakfast. Prisoners in black-and-white bee-striped uniforms gather under the metal-grid stairs and tip dead cockroaches into a trash bin from plastic peanut-butter containers they'd set as traps during the night. All eyes are on me in the chow line. Watching who sits where, I hold my head up, put on a solid stare and pretend to be as at home in this environment as the cockroaches. It's all an act. I'm lonely and afraid. I loathe having to explain myself to the head of the white race, who I assume is the toughest murderer. I've been in jail long enough to know that taking my breakfast to my cell will imply that I have something to hide.

The gang punishes criminals with certain charges. The most serious are sex offenders, who are KOS: Kill On Sight. Other charges are punishable by SOS – Smash On Sight – such as drive-by shootings because women and kids sometimes get killed. It's called convict justice. Gang members are constantly looking for people to beat up because that's how they earn their reputations and tattoos. The most serious acts of violence earn the highest-ranking tattoos. To be a full gang member requires murder. I've observed the body language and techniques inmates trying to integrate employ. An inmate with a spring in his step and an air of confidence is likely to be accepted. A person who avoids eye contact and fails to introduce himself to the gang is likely to be preyed on. Some of the failed attempts I saw ended up with heads getting cracked against toilets, a sound I've grown familiar with. I've seen prisoners being extracted on stretchers who looked dead – one had yellow fluid leaking from his head. The constant violence gives me nightmares, but the reality is that I put myself in here, so I force myself to accept it as a part of my punishment.

It's time to apply my knowledge. With a self-assured stride, I take my breakfast bag to the table of white inmates covered in neo-Nazi tattoos, allowing them to question me.

"Mind if I sit with you guys?" I ask, glad exhaustion has deepened my voice.

"These seats are taken. But you can stand at the corner of the table."

The man who answered is probably the head of the gang. I size him up. Cropped brown hair. A dangerous glint in Nordic-blue eyes. Tiny pupils that suggest he's on heroin. Weightlifter-type veins bulging from a sturdy neck. Political ink on arms crisscrossed with scars. About the same age as me, thirty-three.

"Thanks. I'm Shaun from England." I volunteer my origin to show I'm different from them but not in a way that might get me smashed.

"I'm Bullet, the head of the whites." He offers me his fist to bump. "Where you roll in from, wood?"

Addressing me as wood is a good sign. It's what white gang members on a friendly basis call each other.

"Towers jail. They increased my bond and re-classified me to maximum security."

"What's your bond at?"

"I've got two $750,000 bonds," I say in a monotone. This is no place to brag about bonds.

"How many people you kill, brother?" His eyes drill into mine, checking whether my body language supports my story. My body language so far is spot on.

"None. I threw rave parties. They got us talking about drugs on wiretaps." Discussing drugs on the phone does not warrant a $1.5 million bond. I know and beat him to his next question. "Here's my charges." I show him my charge sheet, which includes conspiracy and leading a crime syndicate – both from running an Ecstasy ring.

Bullet snatches the paper and scrutinises it. Attempting to pre-empt his verdict, the other whites study his face. On edge, I wait for him to respond. Whatever he says next will determine whether I'll be accepted or victimised.

"Are you some kind of jailhouse attorney?" Bullet asks. "I want someone to read through my case paperwork." During our few minutes of conversation, Bullet has seen through my act and concluded that I'm educated – a possible resource to him.

I appreciate that he'll accept me if I take the time to read his case. "I'm no jailhouse attorney, but I'll look through it and help you however I can."

"Good. I'll stop by your cell later on, wood."

After breakfast, I seal as many of the cracks in the walls as I can with toothpaste. The cell smells minty, but the cockroaches still find their way in. Their day shift appears to be collecting information on the brown paper bags under my bunk, containing a few items of food that I purchased from the commissary; bags that I tied off with rubber bands in the hope of keeping the cockroaches out. Relentlessly, the cockroaches explore the bags for entry points, pausing over and probing the most worn and vulnerable regions. *Will the nightly swarm eat right through the paper?* I read all morning, wondering whether my cellmate has died in his cocoon, his occasional breathing sounds reassuring me.

Bullet stops by late afternoon and drops his case paperwork off. He's been charged with Class 3 felonies and less, not serious crimes, but is facing a double-digit sentence because of his prior convictions and Security Threat Group status in the prison system. The proposed sentencing range seems disproportionate. I'll advise him to reject the plea bargain – on the assumption he already knows to do so, but is just seeking the comfort of a second opinion, like many un-sentenced inmates. When he returns for his paperwork, our conversation disturbs my cellmate – the cocoon shuffles – so we go upstairs to his cell. I tell Bullet what I think. He is excitable, a different man from earlier, his pupils almost non-existent.

"This case ain't shit. But my prosecutor knows I done other shit, all kinds of heavy shit, but can't prove it. I'd do anything to get that sorry bitch off my fucking ass. She's asking for something bad to happen to her. Man, if I ever get bonded out, I'm gonna chop that bitch into pieces. Kill her slowly though. Like to work her over with a blowtorch."

Such talk can get us both charged with conspiring to murder a prosecutor, so I try to steer him elsewhere. "It's crazy how they can catch you doing one thing, yet try to sentence you for all of the things they think you've ever done."

"Done plenty. Shot some dude in the stomach once. Rolled him up in a blanket and threw him in a dumpster."

Discussing past murders is as unsettling as future ones. "So, what's all your tattoos mean, Bullet? Like that eagle on your chest?"

"Why you wanna know?" Bullet's eyes probe mine.

My eyes hold their ground. "Just curious."

"It's a war bird. The AB patch."

"AB patch?"

"What the Aryan Brotherhood gives you when you've put enough work in."

"How long does it take to earn a patch?"

"Depends how quickly you put your work in. You have to earn your lightning bolts first."

"Why you got red and black lightning bolts?"

"You get SS bolts for beating someone down or for being an enforcer for the family. Red lightning bolts for killing someone. I was sent down as a youngster. They gave me steel and told me who to handle and I handled it. You don't ask questions. You just get blood on your steel. Dudes who get these tats without putting work in are told to cover them up or leave the yard."

"What if they refuse?"

"They're held down and we carve the ink off them."

Imagining them carving a chunk of flesh to remove a tattoo, I cringe. He's really enjoying telling me this now. His volatile nature is clear and frightening. *He's accepted me too much. He's trying to impress me before making demands.*

At night, I'm unable to sleep. Cocooned in heat, surrounded by cockroaches, I hear the swamp-cooler vent – a metal grid at the top of a wall – hissing out tepid air. Giving up on sleep, I put my earphones on and tune into National Public Radio. Listening to a Vivaldi violin concerto, I close my eyes and press my tailbone down to straighten my back as if I'm doing a yogic relaxation. The playful allegro thrills me, lifting my spirits, but the wistful adagio provokes sad emotions and tears. I open my eyes and gaze into the gloom. Due to lack of sleep, I start hallucinating and hearing voices over the music whispering threats. I'm at breaking point. Although I have accepted that I committed crimes and deserve to be punished, no one should have to live like this. I'm furious at myself for making the series of reckless decisions that put me in here and for losing absolutely everything. As violins crescendo in my ears, I remember what my life used to be like.